FASHION DRAWING

楽しく描く表現テクニック

INTRODUCTION

イントロダクション

　旧版の発行から数年が経過し、この度、新たに筆を加え「新版」化しました。新版化の最大の理由は〝英文、併記〟の必要性を感じたことです。海外からの就労者や留学生は急増し、彼らとの交わりも日常的となりグローバリズムな社会を実感！特に学校現場の教壇に立つと、そうした方々にも供する教材を、との思いを募らせてきました。

　一人ひとりに個性があるように、服に対するイメージや表現の仕方も違います。ファッションをドローイングするということは、自分の考えや伝えたいことを分かるように表わすこと！まさに思考を可視化したものと言えます。アイデアや感じたひらめきを、気持ちのままに描きけるように導きます。

　本書では❶インスピレーションを引き出す自由な表現法❷基本的な人体の法則❸着色法❹デジタル技術を駆使した表現までの4部構成にまとめています。

Several years have passed since the previous edition was published, and this time, I created a "new edition" with adding some ideas. The biggest reason for the new edition was that I have felt that it needs to be written "in English" as well. As the number of international workers and students from overseas has increased rapidly, I have been realizing the global society in a daily routine that has been increasing the interaction with them!! In particular, I have heightened the feelings for providing educational materials to those international people when I stand in front of students in the educational environment. The image of clothes and how to express the clothing are different as same as each person has their own personality. Drawing the fashion means expressing your thoughts and what you want to convey! It can be said that it is a visualization of thought. This book leads you to be able to draw your ideas and inspirations as your heart wishes. This book is organized into four-part: 1. Free expressions to bring out the inspiration, 2. Basic rules of human body, 3. Coloring method, 4. Expression that makes full use of digital technology.

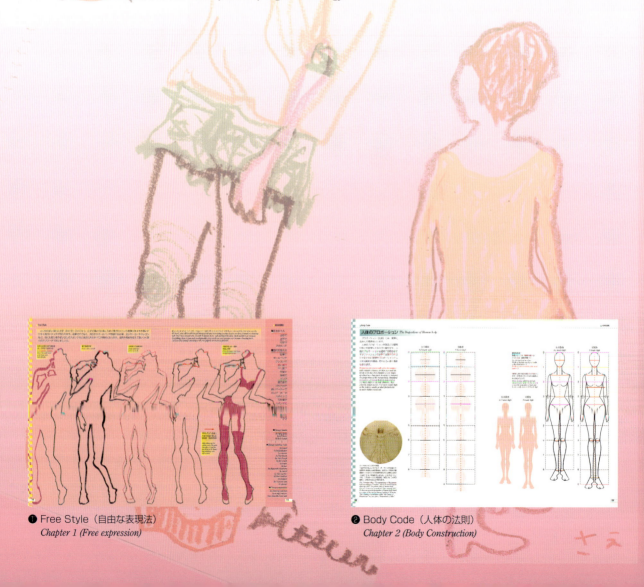

❶ Free Style（自由な表現法）
Chapter 1 (Free expression)

❷ Body Code（人体の法則）
Chapter 2 (Body Construction)

❸ Give Coloring (着色しよう)
Chapter 3 (Try coloring)

❹ Do Photoshop (フォトショップで描く)
Chapter 4 (Draw by Photoshop)

Contents

第1章 フリースタイル（自由な表現法）……6
Chapter 1: Free Style (Free expression)

アウトラインを追いかける……9
With the Outline / Chasing the outline

アウトラインで描く……10
Drawing by outline

画材で変わる線……14
Lines that change depending on the painting tool

持ち方で変わる線……16
Lines that change depending on the grip

ショーケース・1……18
Showcase・1

ショーケース・2……20
Showcase・2

ショーケース・3……22
Showcase・3

ショーケース・4……24
Showcase・4

思いのままに描く……27
With your Imagination / Drawing with imagination

心のままに描く……28
Drawing by following your heart

ぼかし&にじみを使って……33
Using blurring (fading) & bleeding

ぼかし&にじみで描く……32
Drawing by blurring (fading) & bleeding

ショーケース・5……34
Showcase・5

ショーケース・6……36
Showcase・6

ショーケース・7……38
Showcase・7

デカルコマニーで描く……40
Drawing with Decalcomania

ショーケース・8……41
Showcase・8

ショーケース・9……42
Showcase・9

バティックで描く……44
Drawing with Batik

ショーケース・10……45
Showcase・10

ショーケース・11……46
Showcase・11

水彩技法のいろいろ……48
Various watercolor techniques

第2章 ボディコード（人体の法則）……50
Chapter 2: Body Code (Body Construction)

人体のプロポーション……52
The Proportions of Human body

プロポーション（女性）……54
Proportion (Women)

プロポーション（男性）……56
Proportion (Men)

正面片足重心ポーズ（女性）……58
Front pose with center of gravity on one-foot (Women)

正面片足重心ポーズ（男性）……60
Front pose with center of gravity on one-foot (Men)

斜め片足重心ポーズ（女性）……62
Angled pose with center of gravity on one-foot (Women)

斜め片足重心ポーズ（男性）……64
Angled pose with center of gravity on one-foot (Men)

後ろ・横ポーズ（女性／男性）……66
Back・Profile (Side) pose (Women/Men)

顔を描く……68
Drawing a facee

いろいろな角度の顔……70
Faces of various angles

帽子を描く……72
Drawing a hat

手を描く……74
Drawing a hand

いろいろな角度の手……76
Hands of various angles

手と手袋……78
Hands and gloves

足を描く……80
Drawing a foot

靴を描く／側面（ローヒール）……82
Drawing shoes/low heel (Profile/Side)

靴を描く／側面（ハイヒール）……84
Drawing shoes/high heel (Profile/Side)

靴を描く／斜め（ローヒール・ハイヒール）……86
Drawing shoes/high heel (Angled state)

靴を描く／いろいろな角度（ハイヒール）……88
Drawing shoes/high heel (Various angles)

ドレープを描く……90
Drawing a drape

ドレープと柄の動き……92
Movement of drapes and patterns

ポーズバリエーション……94
Pose variation

第3章 ギブカラーリング（着色しよう）……98
Chapter 3: Give Coloring (Try coloring)

水彩で描く………………………………… 102
Drawing with Watercolor

ショートヘアを描く／目を描く………… 104
Drawing Short hair / Drawing Eyes

ミディアムヘアを描く／口を描く……… 105
Drawing Medium hair / Drawing a Mouth

ロングヘアを描く………………………… 106
Drawing Long hair

単色で立体感を出す……………………… 108
Creating a three-dimensional effect for a single color

透ける素材を描く………………………… 110
Drawing Transparent materials/fabrics

モアレ模様を描く………………………… 112
Drawing the Moiré Pattern

エナメルを描く…………………………… 114
Drawing the Enamel

ヘリンボーンを描く……………………… 116
Drawing the pattern of Herringbone

ラメ素材を描く…………………………… 118
Drawing the Lamé (Glitter) materials/fabrics

千鳥格子を描く…………………………… 120
Drawing the pattern of Houndstooth

ファーを描く……………………………… 122
Drawing the Fur

マーカーで描く…………………………… 124
Drawing with Marker

濃・中・淡で立体感を出す……………… 126
Creating a three-dimensional effect with shade in dark, medium and light

色を重ねてニットを描く………………… 128
Drawing the Knit fabric by layering colors

いろいろな画材で描く…………………… 130
Drawing with Various Painting Tools

ウォーム素材を描く……………………… 132
Drawing Warm materials/fabrics

レザーを描く……………………………… 134
Drawing the Leather

シャイニング素材を描く………………… 136
Drawing Shining materials/fabrics

さまざまな画材の組み合わせ…………… 138
Combination of various painting tools/materials

ギャラリー・1 …………………………… 140
Gallery・1

ギャラリー・2 …………………………… 142
Gallery・2

第4章 ドゥフォトショップ（フォトショップで描く）… 142
Chapter 4: Drawing with Photoshop

色について………………………………… 146
Colors

Photoshopのツールボックス…………… 148
Tools Panel in Photoshop

Photoshopのパネル……………………… 149
Other Panels in Photoshop

Photoshopの画面と名称………………… 150
Workspace in Photoshop and Names of its Elements

フィルターで素材づくり………………… 151
Creating Textures with Filters

フィルターで作る凹凸素材とウオッシュデニム…152
Creating a Rough Texture and Washed Denim Texture with Filters

フィルターで作るボーダー、ストライプ、チェック…154
Creating Stripe and Check Patterns with Filters

フィルターと「グラデーション」で作る型押しパイソン… 156
Creating a Python-Embossed Leather Texture Using Filters and Gradient

フィルターと「カスタムシェイプ」で作るラバープリント… 158
Creating A Rubber Print Texture Using Filters and Custom Shape

フィルターと「グラデーションマップ」で作るレオパード… 160
Creating a Leopard Texture with Filters and Gradient Map

素材をデザイン画にマッピング………… 163
Adding Patterns and Textures to Clothing

「拡大・縮小」と「コピースタンプツール」で素材をマッピング… 164
Adding a pattern to clothing with Scale and Clone Stamp

「自動選択ツール」で選択「色相・彩度」で色を変える… 166
Selecting and Changing a Color Using Magic Wand Tool and Hue/Saturation

「パターンの定義」と「変形」でマッピング……… 168
Adding a Texture to Clothing with Define Pattern and Transform

スキャン画像を「レベル補正」で調整…………… 170
Adjusting a Scanned Image with Levels

「ブラシプリセット」でプリント柄…………… 172
Creating a Print Texture with Brush Settings

「ペンタブレット」で描く……………………… 174
Using a Pen Tablet

「レイヤーマスク」でマスキングする………… 178
Masking out Part of an Image with a Layer Mask

「パターンを定義」で連続柄……………………… 180
Masking out Part of an Image with a Layer Mask

「レイヤースタイル」で特殊効果を加える……… 182
Masking out Part of an Image with a Layer Mask

イメージを伝える………………………………… 185
Telling Your Image

「イラストモデル」をレイヤーでカラーバリエーション… 186
Creating Color Variations of a Model Illustration with Layers

「デザイン提案イラスト」作成の手順…………… 188
Procedure for Creating a Design Proposal Illustration

「文字ツール」でタイトルを作成する…………… 192
Creating a Title with the Type Tool

「デザイン提案イラスト」を仕上げる…………… 194
Completing the Illustration

「インビテーション・カード」を作成する 196
Creating an Invitation Card

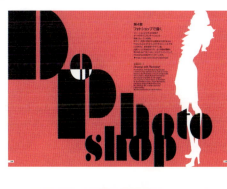

第1章
自由な表現法

真っ白な紙を前にして、いざ描くとなると
ドキドキ戸惑うのではないでしょうか？
うまく描かなければ！という思いにとらわれず
大胆にアウトラインを追いかけましょう。
自由な発想で描くことで
思わぬイメージや面白いフォルムに出会い
初めて描く人も、描き慣れている人も
新たな発見やアイデアを得て
とても個性的で楽しい仕上がりになります。

Chapter 1
Free Style (Free expression)

Don't you feel uncomfortable and nervous when it comes to painting and you have your white paper in front of you? Without getting caught up in "I have to draw well!"-thoughts, you can chase the outline in a bold manner. Both beginners and people who are accustomed to drawing can encounter unexpected images, interesting shapes, make discoveries and get new ideas, which will result in a very original and fun finish when drawing free style.

With the
Outline

アウトラインを追いかける

絵を描くのが下手！苦手！おっくう！と思っていませんか！?
そんな苦手意識がアウトラインを追いかけるだけで
あっという間に楽しく描けるようになります
うまくはないけれど味が出て良い感じ！
外側のラインを探していろいろな画材を使い
新たな自分を発見しましょう

Chasing the outline

I am not good at drawing! Not good at all!
It's so troublesome!
Isn't that what you are thinking?
This feeling can be changed by only following
the outline and it makes drawing fun in a heartbeat.
It might not be a great skill,
but it will create a nice feeling of originality.
Let's look for the outlines and find our new,
own style by using various drawing tools.

■ Free Style

アウトラインで描く *Drawing by outline*

　アウトライン（輪郭線・シルエット）とは、空間と立体とを分けているラインです。目の前の対象を見て、どこから描いてよいのか戸惑うことはないでしょうか？　眼に飛び込んでくる情報の中からアウトラインのみに集中して描くことで、面白い線に出会ったり案外その本質をとらえて、絵を描くことの怖さがなくなります。洋服の分量感やシルエットを素早くとらえることにもつながります。

The outline (outline, silhouette) is a line that separates an object and the space that the object exists in. Have you ever wondered where to start drawing when seeing the actual object right in front of you? Out of all the information that jumps into your eyes when seeing the object, focusing only on the outline will let your fear for drawing fade as you encounter interesting lines and catch the object's essence. It also helps understanding the volume and silhouette of garments quickly.

いったん描き始めたら手を離さずに最後まで輪郭を追いかけます

Do not set down the pen and follow the outline to the end once you have starting drawing.

Photographer 加藤智恵子・Stylist 高田いづみ
Hair&Make-up 江黒美香・Model 松下未奈

Free Style

いつもの使い慣れた右手（利き手）だけでなく、左手で描いてみるとうまく描きたいという意識がなくなり思いがけなく面白いタッチが得られます。鉛筆だけでなく、滑らかなボールペンや強弱の出る筆、太いマーカーやクレヨンなど。他にも割り箸や使い古しのスポンジなど身近にあるすべてが画材になります。道具や用紙を変えて思いつく限りのアプローチで試しましょう。

左手と右手に違う画材を持って両手で描きます
Use separate drawing tools for each hand and draw with both hands.

筆で描きます
Draw with a brush.

2本持って描きます
Draw with two painting tools.

If you try to draw not only using your right (dominant) hand, which you are used to, but also use the left hand, you will be able to get unexpected and interesting touches as you are less focused on drawing well. Don't use only pencils, smooth ballpoint pens, soft and hard brushes, thick markers or crayons. Everything close to you such as disposable chop sticks or used sponges can become drawing tools. Let's try and change drawing tools and papers as much as possible.

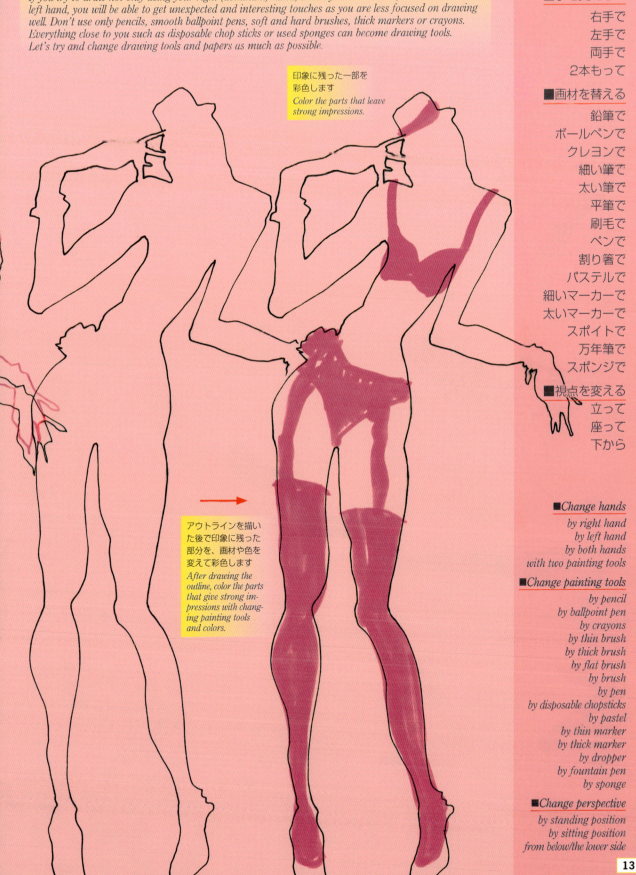

印象に残った一部を
彩色します
Color the parts that leave strong impressions.

アウトラインを描い
た後で印象に残った
部分を、画材や色を
変えて彩色します
After drawing the outline, color the parts that give strong impressions with changing painting tools and colors.

自由な表現法

■手を変える
右手で
左手で
両手で
2本もって

■画材を替える
鉛筆で
ボールペンで
クレヨンで
細い筆で
太い筆で
平筆で
刷毛で
ペンで
割り箸で
パステルで
細いマーカーで
太いマーカーで
スポイトで
万年筆で
スポンジで

■視点を変える
立って
座って
下から

■Change hands
by right hand
by left hand
by both hands
with two painting tools

■Change painting tools
by pencil
by ballpoint pen
by crayons
by thin brush
by thick brush
by flat brush
by brush
by pen
by disposable chopsticks
by pastel
by thin marker
by thick marker
by dropper
by fountain pen
by sponge

■Change perspective
by standing position
by sitting position
from below/the lower side

■ Free Style

画材で変わる線 Lines that change depending on the painting tool

線は画材によってさまざまな表情を見せてくれます。筆や色鉛筆など柔らかい道具で描くとやさしく柔らかい線に、ペンや割り箸など硬い道具で描くと強く硬い線になります。

Lines show different expressions with different painting tools. Lines drawn with soft tools such as brushes or colored pencils will become soft and gentle, whereas lines drawn with hard tools such as pens or disposable chopsticks will become hard and strong.

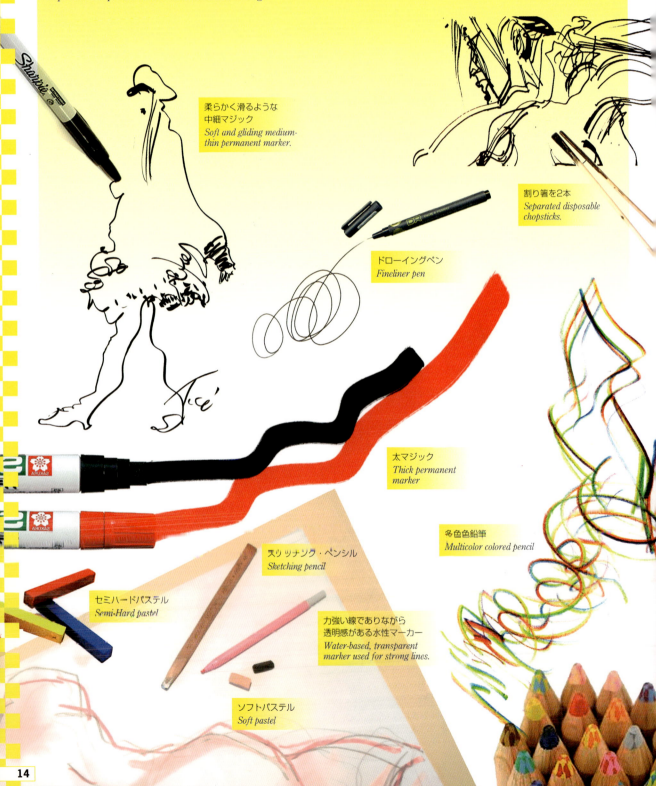

柔らかく滑るような中細マジック
Soft and gliding medium-thin permanent marker.

割り箸を2本
Separated disposable chopsticks.

ドローイングペン
Fineliner pen

太マジック
Thick permanent marker

多色色鉛筆
Multicolor colored pencil

スケッチング・ペンシル
Sketching pencil

セミハードパステル
Semi-Hard pastel

力強い線でありながら透明感がある水性マーカー
Water-based, transparent marker used for strong lines.

ソフトパステル
Soft pastel

自由な表現法

刷毛
Brush

割り箸
Disposable chopsticks

太い線と鋭利な線が面白いコーラペン
Folded pen that has interesting thick lines and sharp lines.

墨汁
Indian ink

色鉛筆
Colored pencil

丸ペン
Mapping pen

穂先をカットした筆
Brush with cut-tip.

柔らかい筆
Soft brush

15

Free Style

持ち方で変わる線 *Lines that change depending on the grip*

　線は持つ位置や角度、力の入れ方、握り方によって軽く柔らかいタッチから力強いタッチまでさまざまな質感が生まれます。画材の特徴を生かしながらいろいろ試してみましょう。

Depending on the position, angle and force of the grip, various textures from light and soft touches to strong touches can be created. Let's try different things while making use of the characteristics of the painting tools.

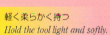
自由な表現法

基本的な持ち方
Basic way of holding.

軽く柔らかく持つ
Hold the tool light and softly.

両手で力強く握る
Hold the tool firmly by both hands.

寝かせて持つ
Hold the tool with a tilt.

短く持つ
Hold the tool close to the tip.

短く軽く持つ
Hold the tool loosely and close to the tip.

長く軽く持つ
Hold the tool loosely and far from the tip.

短く握って持つ
Hold the tool firmly and close to the lip.

17

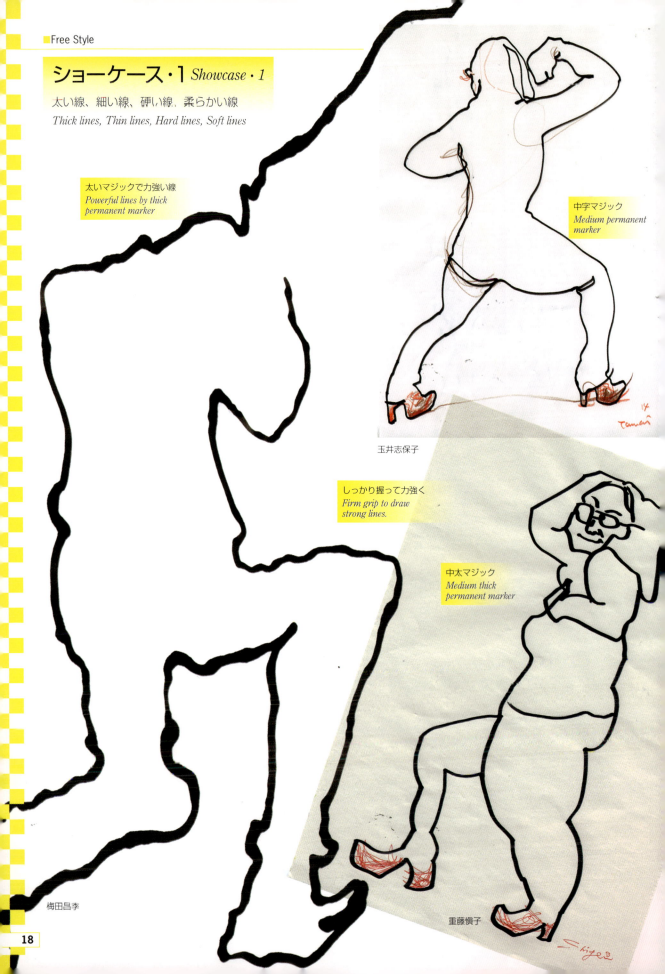

自由な表現法

寝かせて持って
柔らかい線
Soft lines by using a tool at a tilt

マジック＋色鉛筆
Permanent marker + colored pencil

ドローイングペン＋
油性マーカー
Drawing pen + oil-based marker

19

■ Free Style

ショーケース・2 *Showcase · 2*
パステルやクレヨンの伸びやかな柔らかい線
Soft, relaxing and lively lines by using pastels and crayons

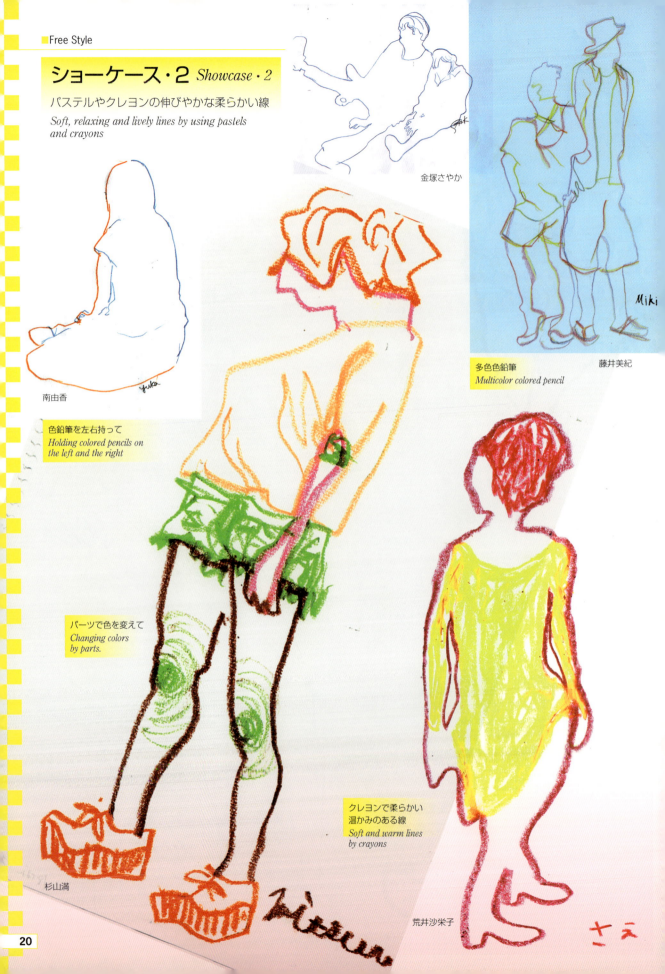

色鉛筆を左右持って
Holding colored pencils on the left and the right

南由香

金塚さやか

多色色鉛筆
Multicolor colored pencil

藤井美紀

パーツで色を変えて
Changing colors by parts.

クレヨンで柔らかい温かみのある線
Soft and warm lines by crayons

杉山満

荒井沙栄子

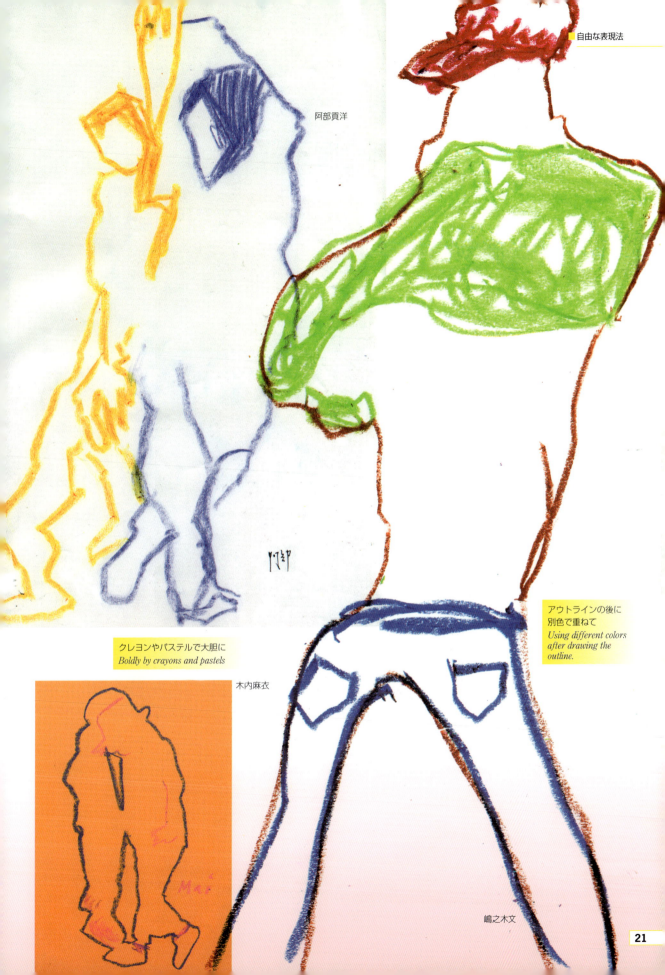

自由な表現法

阿部貢洋

クレヨンやパステルで大胆に
Boldly by crayons and pastels

木内麻衣

アウトラインの後に別色で重ねて
Using different colors after drawing the outline.

嶋之木文

■ Free Style

ショーケース・3 *Showcase・3*
一部を彩色する、2本持って描く
Coloring partially, drawing by using two painting tools.

鈴木結

兼田多鶴子

ドローイングペンの先端を持ってゆらゆらとしたアウトライン
Drawing shaky outlines by holding the edge of the drawing pen

阿部貢洋

富永明日香

リディクジックに色鉛筆で彩色
Coloring with colored pencils onto medium permanent marker

仲松あかね

22

■自由な表現法

紅陽

ボールペン2本の同時使い！うんと離して持つと面白い形状に
Using two ballpoint pens simultaneously. It becomes an interesting shape when holding the tools with a fair distance from another.

辻なつか

2色の色鉛筆の同時使いで思いがけない立体感
Unexpected 3D aspect by simultaneous use of 2 colored

重藤愼子

仲松あかね

マーカーで柔らかく大胆に
Soft and boldly by using markers

衣笠理子

23

■ Free Style

ショーケース・４ *Showcase・4*
色紙に描く、一部を彩色、画材を変えて描く

Drawing on colored paper, coloring partially,
drawing with changing painting tools.

藤井美紀

森本麻友

南真帆

平野麻理恵

井上綾夏

南真帆

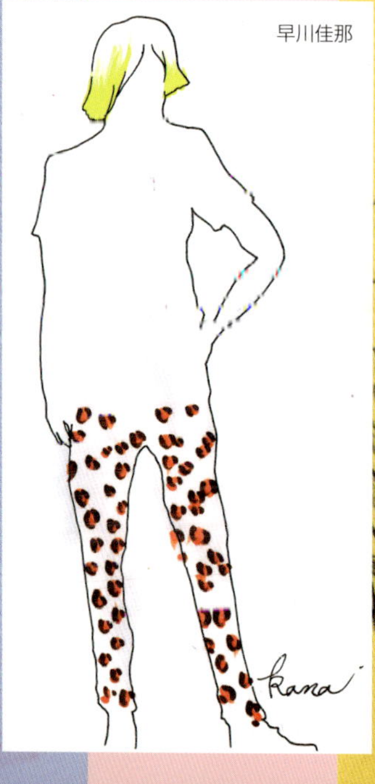

早川佳那

■ 自由な表現法

パステルで一部彩色
Coloring partially using pastel.

安田菜

松井祐也

藤井琴美

五寶雅美

平野麻理恵

南真帆

木内麻衣

原澤優衣

25

With your
Imagination

思いのままに描く

何かを意図して描こうとするのではなく
自分の心のままに色をおき筆を走らせ
最後に形にしていく方法です！
偶然の結果や無意識に描くことで
思いがけない発見があり
新しいデザインの発想につながります

Drawing with imagination

Instead of trying to draw intentionally,
with this method the shape will form
at the very end after running brushes
and colors freely following only your mind.
This connects to new design ideas,
as accidental results and unexpected ideas can be
found by drawing unconsciously.

■ Free Style

心のままに描く *Drawing by following your heart*

　個人の考えよりも、無意識や集団の意識、偶然を利用して造形化するという技法や手法があります。その日の気持ちや心の動きのままにカタチを定めず、色をぼかしたり、飛ばしたり、にじませたり自由に描いていくと思いがけない形が現われます。斜めにしたり、逆さにしたり、引いてみたり、拡大してみたり…いろいろな形が見えてきませんか。

There are approaches and techniques that make use of the unconsciousness, group consciousness and chance rather than individual thinking. Unplanned forms will appear if you if you blur, splash and bleed colors without deciding the form beforehand, or freely draw by following your feelings and your state of mind of the day. Try to shift it diagonally, upside down, pull and expand it ...
Can you see the various shapes?

みんなでコラボ……
Collaborating with everyone ....

別々に描いて合わせてみます
Drawing separately and trying to combine.

紙を破って上から置いて……
Draw a big eye on other papers and put on top

■ 自由な表現法

紙を立てて絵の具をたらして
Drip colors and make it to bleed

別紙に大きな目々描いて置いてみる
Trying to draw big eyes on a separate paper.

色をぽたぽた落としてにじませる
Dripping colors and bleeding it

筆をはじいて絵の具を飛ばして
Flicking brushes and splashing

上から絵の具を
ぽたぽたと
Dripping paint from above.

転写して描き加えて
Transcribing and adding.

■ Free Style

ぼかし&にじみを使って *Using blurring (fading) & bleeding*

　いつもの描さなれた手順ではなく、その日の気持ちや心の動きのままに色をぼかしたり、飛ばしたり、にじませたりと自由に描きます。充分乾かして斜めにしたり、逆さにしたり、引いてみたり、拡大してみましょう。いろいろな形が見えてきます。次に別の紙に大きな顔や小さな顔を描き、元の絵と合わせてみてください。縦に置いたり横にして置くだけでさまざまなデザインが見えてきます。

Drawing freely by making use of blurring, splashing and bleeding colors by following your feelings and state of mind of the day instead of following the usual drawing procedure. After adequate drying, let's try and shift the piece diagonally, upside down, try pull and expand it. Various forms will appear. Then draw a big or small face on a separate paper and try to combine it with the original picture. Just by placing it vertically or horizontally you can see various designs.

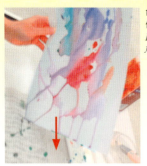

色を自由に置いて、たらしたり、ぼかしたり
偶然との出会いを楽しみましょう
Let's enjoy chance encounters, by putting colors freely, dripping and blurring.

充分に乾いたあとで、角度を変えてみるといろいろなフォルムが見えてきます。
After it's dry enough, you can see various shapes by changing the angle.

原画　*Original drawing*

横にして……
Make it horizontally…

斜めにして……
Make it diagonally…

縦にして……
Make it vertically…

逆さにして……
Make it upside down…

■ 自由な表現法

横にしたり斜めにしたり……
Make it horizontally and/or diagonally…

大きな顔を合わせてシャポーに……
Make it a chapeau by combining with a big face…

小さな顔を合わせるとドレスに見えたり……
It looks like a dress by combining with a small face…

別紙に顔や手を描いて
合わせてみます
*Draw faces and/or hands
on a separate sheet,
and try to combine it.*

31

■ Free Style

ぼかし&にじみで描く *Drawing by blurring (fading) & bleeding*

紙に水を引いて、その上に色を重ねて塗ると自然ににじんで色が広がります。単色でも、また別色を重ねても自然なぼかしやにじみで思いがけない結果を得ることができます。水をたっぷり含ませ引いた上に絵の具を多めにたらします。絵の具を多めにたらし、筆はやや寝かせ気味にして描くのがコツです。

If you apply water onto the paper and apply color over it, it will naturally bleed and spread. You can get unexpected results with natural bleeding and blurring whether you are using single colors or different colors for layering. The key to using this technique well is using plenty of water and paint, and a slight tilt of the brush.

自由に描いた形を乾かします。別紙に大きな顔や小さな顔を描き縦にしたり横にするだけでさまざまな形が見えてきます
Freely draw a shape and let it dry, you can see various shapes just by drawing a big or small face on a separate paper and putting it next to it vertically or horizontally.

顔を小さく描くとベストに見えたり
It looks like a vest if you draw a small face.

上下を逆にするとドレスに見えたり……
It looks like a dress if you turn it upside down…

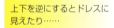

横にすると帽子に見えたり……
It looks like a hat if you put it horizontally……

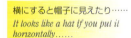

■ 自由な表現法

うまく描かなくては！との思いにとらわれず偶然との出会いに身を任せることで、思い切ったタッチで描くことができます
Without getting caught up in the "I have to draw well!"-thought, you can draw with a bold touch by leaving it up to chance.

水をたっぷり含ませて引きます
Apply plenty of water onto the paper.

絵の具を濃いめに落とします
Apply paint deeply.

自然なにじみが広がります
The paint starts to naturally blur and bleed.

絵の具を足していきます
Add some more.

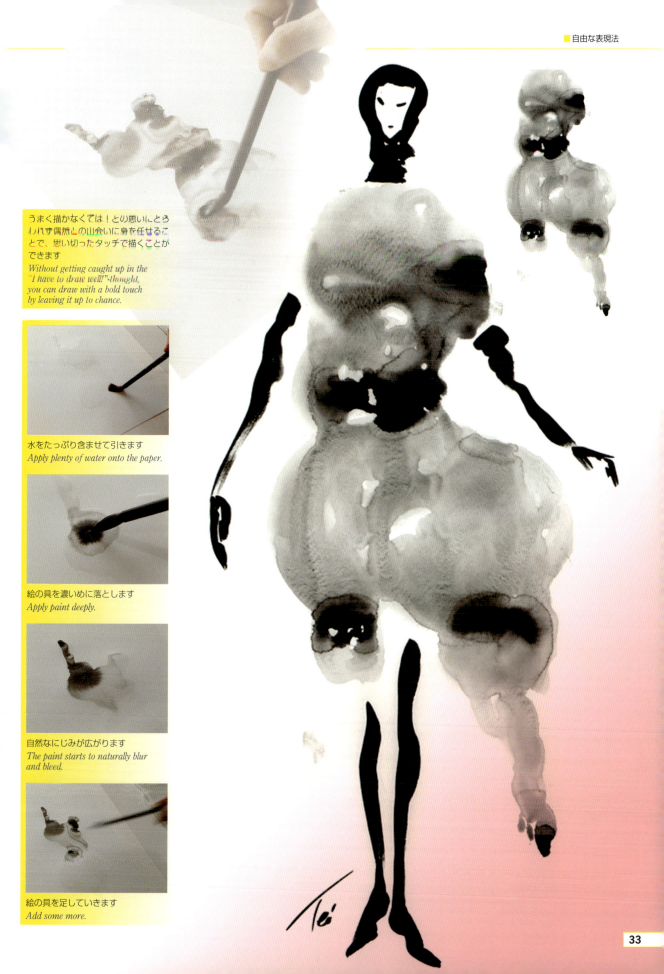

33

■ Free Style

ショーケース・5 *Showcase・5*

水彩の水量を生かして描く

Drawing with using huge amounts of water in watercolor.

大きな筆で大胆ににじませた。フォルムをそのまま生かした楽しくワイルドなシルエット！
A wild yet delightful silhouette is created by using bold blurring with a big brush.

吉峯晶子

水彩をたらした後に、息を吹きかけて絵の具を吹き散らして描いたジャイアントシャポー
A giant chapeau painted by blowing and splashing paint after dripping watercolor onto the paper.

梅田昌季

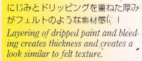

にじみとドリッピングを重ねた厚みがフェルトのような素材感に！
Layering of dripped paint and bleeding creates thickness and creates a look similar to felt texture.

黄孟夢

34

■ 自由な表現法

スパッタリングのテクスチャーと色鉛筆を生かしてデリケートなテキスタイルのドレスを表現
Expression of a delicate textile dress by using sputter art texture and color pencils.

大久保省吾

絵の具のチューブをそのまま紙面に塗りつけ、上から水をおいて、紙を動かしながら水彩をたらした大胆で面白い発想
A bold and interesting idea, created by putting paint onto the paper directly from the tube and then spreading it by dripping water on top of it and moving the paper.

小瀬堅太

にじみやぼかしと繊細なラインでコントラスをつけてグローブに表現した2人のコラボレーション
Collaboration work by two people, who expressed a glove by contrasting blurring and bleeding with delicate lines.

中島あずさ＆松永薫

35

■ Free Style

ショーケース・6 *Showcase・6*
太い筆のタッチを生かして大胆に描く
Drawing boldly by using the touch of thick brushes.

水を切ってドライにした状態の刷毛で描いた。タッチをそのまま生かし、リズミカルにラインを重ねてシャポーに展開

Drawn with a completely dry brush, then developed into a chapeau by using the touch as it is and layering the lines rhythmically.

後藤亜希子

丸筆で色を重ねた。混色の塊がドレスの袖にも見えたり、方向を変えるとクラッチバックのようにも、光沢のあるビーズの塊のようにも見える

The colors are being overlapped with a round paint brush. The mixed color cluster loos like a dress sleeve, and when rotated it looks like a clutch bag or a block of shiny beads.

尾林大樹

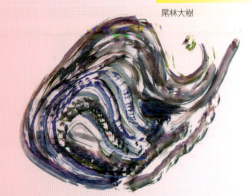

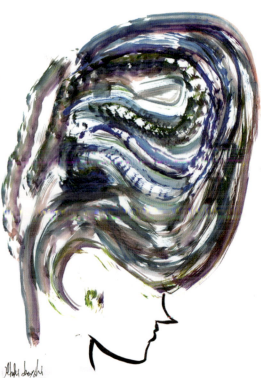

■ 自由な表現法

刷毛で落書きのように自由に描いた量感たっぷりの大胆なシルエットのコートドレス
Drawn with a brush and by freehand, this graffiti-like, bold silhouette with plenty of texture expresses a coat dress.
立石明

絵の具をたっぷり含ませた極太の筆で勢いよく描いた。立体的で存在感のあるタッチがそのままアバンギャルドなフォルムのドレスに！
Drawn vigorously with a thick brush containing several paints. The three-dimensional style and touch that has a sense of presence becomes an avant-garde shaped dress.
金成河

大きな筆に絵の具をたっぷり含ませ、にじみ、ぼかし、かすれを生かして描いた。最後に繊細な面相筆でストラップを加え、バレーシューズに！始めから意図しては描けないタッチ
Drawn by using blurring, bleeding and scratching with a big brush containing several paints. The strap is added with a fine-point brush to create ballet shoes. This is a touch that cannot intentionally be drawn with the idea in mind from the beginning.
細谷修

作：細谷修

■ Free Style

ショーケース・7 *Showcase・7*
いろいろな筆の特徴を生かして描く
Drawing by making use of the different characteristics of brushes.

書道用の極太筆で春夏秋冬の文字を描き、ドレスに表現した作品
This artwork shows dresses made by writing the Chinese characters for spring, summer, autumn and winter. An extra thick brush for calligraphy was used.

福沢明日香

何色もの絵の具をドライなタッチで点描風に直接重ねて描いた。ぼかしで軽い質感に仕上げたトップスとボリューム感のあるボトムスとの対比が美しいドレス！
Drawn by layering many paint colors with a dry touch like a pointillism. This dress shows a beautiful contrast between the voluminous bottom and the top finish with a light texture using blur.

畑山夏美

広い面を塗る平筆、線や細かい模様を描く時に使う丸筆や面相筆。それぞれの筆の特徴がタッチに生かされた軽やかなドレス
Flat brushes are used for coloring the big surface area, round paint brushes and fine point brushes are used for the lines and fine patterns. This light dress shows the use of characteristics of touches for different brushes.

内田智美

■ 自由な表現法

たっぷりの水を含ませた太い丸筆で描いた。リズミカルに叩きつけるようなタッチを生かして大胆なフォルムの作品に！
Drawn with a thick round brush containing plenty of water, this bold shaped artwork is using a rhythmic touch, like flicking brushes.

安田美智子

水滴をたらすようにラインを描いた。その上から太い筆で回すように円を描き加え、透明感のあるドレスに表現
The lines are drawn to look like dripping water. This transparent dress is expressed by adding circles which are drawn by spinning a thick brush.

吉沢智美

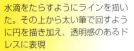

刷毛を使ってドライブラシで揺らぐように一気に描き上げた。波打たせたタッチが存在感のあるシューズに仕上がっている
The lines are drawn to look like dripping water. This transparent dress is expressed by adding circles which are drawn by spinning a thick brush.

山崎翔平

39

■Free Style

デカルコマニーで描く *Drawing with Decalcomania*

デカルコマニーとは、フランス語で「転写法・転写方式 転写画」を意味する用語です。2つ折りした紙と紙の間に絵の具を挟み、上から手などでこすった後ゆっくり開くと、左右対称(シンメトリー)の形態が現われます。元々は紙に描いた絵を陶器やガラスに転写し絵付けするための技法ですが、画家のオスカー・ドミンゲスがこの技法を作品に取り入れ、シュールリアリストの画家達に一つの手法として広がりました。描き手のコントロールや意識に関係なく偶然に表れたイメージをデザインに落とし込んでいきます。

The term "Decalcomania" means "transfer method", "transfer system" or "transfer image" in French. A symmetric shape appears when paint is applied onto paper, which is then folded into two and rubbed together and then opened again. Originally, this technique was used to transfer paintings from paper to porcelain or glass, but the artist Oscar Dominguez incorporated the method into his works and it spread as a technique to surrealist painters. It is created without control or intent from the artist and made into a design.

❶片面に自由に絵の具をのせます
Put paint freely on one side.

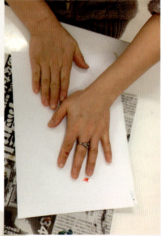

❷もう片面に写し込むように抑えます
Press and rub for transferring the paint to the other side.

❸開くとシンメトリーに絵が移し込まれて思いがけない絵柄が表れます
When opening the folded paper, the transferred image creates an unexpected pattern of symmetry.

伊折淑子

20世紀のシュールレアリズムのドイツ人画家「マックス・エルンスト」の作品。2枚の紙を使って絵の具が伸びた跡など、偶然の形の上に人間や建物、空が描き加えられしいます

Artwork from German surrealist painter Max Ernst of the 20th century. Elements such as people, buildings and the sky are added on the unexpected shapes, like the traces of stretched paint, created by using two paper sheets.

40

▮ 自由な表現法

ショーケース・8 *Showcase・8*

絵の具のチューブをたっぷり塗りつけて転写

Transfer by applying plenty of paint from tubes directly

眼を描き加えて可愛い仮面（マスケラ）ハーフマスクにデザイン

A cute mask (Maschera) drawn by adding eyes afterwards.

岡田侑真

縦、横と何ヵ所ものデカルコマニーで表現した作品。偶然にポンパドールの髪型に見えた部分を生かし2人の女性の舞台衣装のように

This artwork uses many decalcomania placed vertically and horizontally. Finalized as stage costumes for two women, using the part that looks like a pompadour hairstyle.

荒居 歩

41

■ Free Style

ショーケース・9 *Showcase・9*

絵り具を濃くといて濃淡を生かした転写
Transfer by using dark and light textures and paint colors.

結城穂奈美

左右対称に転写されたデカルコマニーのカラフルな模様がキュートなドレスや帽子に！
This colorful, symmetrically transfered decalcomania pattern becomes a cute dress.

荻原しのぶ

庄司真苗

多色で複雑なデカルコマニーのフォルムをセクシーなハイヒールのデザインに
This multi-colored, complicated decalcomania shape is made into a sexy high heel design.

高山佳奈

絵の具のマチエールを生かしてボリュームのあるコートやグローブに表現
The voluminous coat and gloves are expressed using the texture of the paint.

和田佳穂

42

■ 自由な表現法

コラボレーション *Collaboration*
共同作業で新発想のデザインを
Designing new ideas through joint work

シンメトリーな手や足、眼をデカルコマニー（転写）で表現
Symmetrical hands, feet and eyes expressed by the decalcomania technique.

デカルコマニーの後にデザインを施す。左右の絵を2人で各々が担当し仕上げたコラボ作品
Collaboration work done by designing the right and left side separately after using the decalcomania technique.

森大起＆藤岡亜希子

■ Free Style

バティックで描く *Drawing with Batik*

クレヨンなど油性の画材で描き、その上から絵の具を塗ってはじかせて描く方法です。油性で描かれた部分は水をはじき濃い地のベースに明るい模様や素材感を簡単に表現することができます。「バティック」とは、ロウが染料をはじく効果を利用した技法で染められた布のことを指しています。20世紀の初め頃インドネシアのジャワ語がそのまま英語に取り込まれ現在のbatikという言葉として残りました。

This drawing technique utilizes the water-shedding characteristics of oil-based paint materials such as crayons by applying paint on top of it. The oil-based part of the paint repels water and can easily express bright patterns and textures on a dark base. "Batik" is a technique where wax-resistant dyeing is applied to whole cloth or the whole cloth is made using the technique. The word "Batik" is Javanese (Indonesian) and was translated directly into English when it was introduced at the beginning of the 20th century.

濃地のベースにも明るい模様が簡単に表現できます
Even on a dark base it is easy to express bright patterns.

クレヨンで自由に描き、その上から水溶性絵の具で描くとクレヨンで描いた部分がはじけます
Water-based paint on top of a free drawing with crayons. The parts drawn with crayons repel the water-based paint.

注：アクリル系の油性絵の具は弾かないので必ず水溶性の絵の具を使用します。
Note: Acrylic oil-based paint does not repel, so be sure to use water-based paint.

■ 自由な表現法

ショーケース・10 *Showcase・10*

絵の具をたっぷり塗ると、はじく効果がハッキリ出ます。
The repelling effect will appear clearly if you use a lot of water-based paint.

幾何学柄や葉脈をクレヨンで描さ刷毛で絵の具を塗ってシンプルでモダンなテキスタイルに！
A simple and modern textile created by panting with a thick brush on top of geometric patterns and leaf veins made using crayons.

古川里絵

クレヨンの開放的な持ち味と、はみ出した絵の具がデザインに生かされた楽しい作品
This fun piece is designed using the characteristic openness of crayons and overflowing outlines with paint.

モンテローラ　マリアミカエラ

濃淡や強弱のない素朴なクレヨンの特徴を生かした自由で！陽気で！インパクトのあるメンズTシャツ。濃い地のガッシュ（不透明水彩）でフラットな塗り絵感覚が効果的
This free style drawing takes advantage of the crayons without using shading or any sense of intensity and makes for a playful men's t-shirt with impact. The flat coloring touch is applied onto a dark base color using Gouache (opaque watercolor).

桜井洋平

45

■ Free Style

ショーケース・11 Showcase・11

濃淡をつけて塗ることで立体的な表現に。
Three-dimensional expressions made by using different thicknesses.

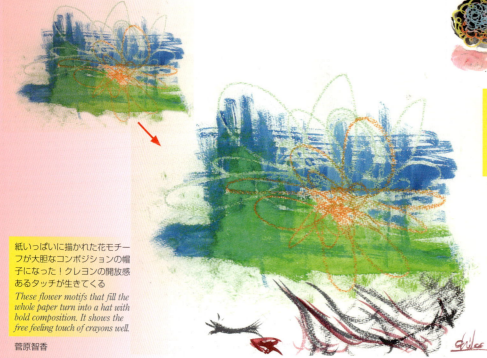

紙いっぱいに描かれた花モチーフが大胆なコンポジションの帽子になった！クレヨンの開放感あるタッチが生きてくる
These flower motifs that fill the whole paper turn into a hat with bold composition. It shows the free feeling touch of crayons well.

菅原智香

曲線を細かくエンドレスにつなげると、いつのまにかふわふわのカーリーニットのソックスに
Without the intention to do so, connecting the detailed curves continuously creates fluffy knit socks.

直井香菜実

手をなぞったリアルな表現もクレヨンで描くとあたたかみが……
Even when actually tracing the shape of a hand, drawing with crayons creates more warmth...

金春霊

すべるように描けるクレヨンの楽しさを生かして描いた帽子。黄色のクレヨンと水彩とのカラーオンカラーで異素材効果！
This hat is drawn using the fun characteristic of crayons enabling a smooth drawing style. It shows different material effects by using color on color with yellow crayons and watercolor.

小林愛

■ 自由な表現法

バティック本来の染料のはじく効果を最大限に生かした。緻密な更紗調のスカートもクレヨンで自由に表現

This piece makes use of the repellent effect of batik to the full extend. A precise chintz-like skirt is expressed freely with crayons.

星野佳世

半円形を重ね波のように反復させた伝統文様「青海波」をクレヨンで描いてキュートなデザインに

This cute design using crayons is made by using the traditional pattern "Ao (Blue), Umi (Sea), Nami (Wave)", which repeats and overlaps semicircles to express a wavy look.

千葉真美

ふわふわとしたヘアリーな軽いニットドレス！メイクやヘアーを強いタッチで描くことで柔らかい素材感を強調

A light knit dress with a fluffy, hairy texture. By drawing the hair and make up with a strong touch, the soft texture of the dress is highlighted.

安明充

カリグラフィー調の文字を描いた上に真っ黒なガッシュを塗り込めて斬新なデザインの帽子に

This hat with an outrageous design is made by applying lots of black gouache onto the calligraphy-style letters.

ステファニー

47

■ Free Style

水彩技法のいろいろ *Various watercolor techniques.*

　第1章では心のおもむくままに描いてきましたが、その中にもいろいろな技法が駆使されています。絵の具（透明・不透明）や紙の種類（荒目、中目、細目）、水の量、乾くタイミングによってさまざまな表情を見せてくれます。水の性質を生かした色のにじみ、ぼかし、かすれなど水と絵の具がおりなす表現が技法につながっているのです。（紙についてはP103参照）

You have tried drawing freely by following your mind in the first chapter, but various techniques were used in the process without intention. Depending on the type of paint and paper, the amount of water used and the timing of the drying various expressions can be shown. The various watercolor techniques that are introduced here are connected to the expressions that can be shown using the characteristics of water such as color blurring, bleeding and scratching.

■ウォッシュ
　水をたっぷりと含ませて広い面をうす塗りする水彩技法の基本です。
■Washing
This basic technique makes use of brushes which contain plenty of water to tint large areas.

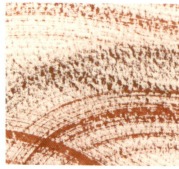

■ドライブラシ
　水気を切った（抑えた）状態で筆を走らせたタッチのことです。かすれた筆触（乾筆）で様々な質感を出すのに効果的です。
■Dry-brush
It is the brush touch created by using the dried (less water) brush. It is effective for creating various textures with scratchy texture of the brush (dry brush). Rough paper, sizing paper (blurring-proof) paper is suitable.

■ウェット・オン・ドライ
　乾いた色の上にまた色を重ねて塗る技法。パレット上で色を混ぜるより彩度が落ちにくく、深みのある色合いが得られます。
■Wet-on-dry
This technique overlaps paint when applied on top of dried color. It does not lose chromatic value as easily as mixed colors on a palette and therefore gives a richer color effect.

■ウェット・オン・ウェット
　濡れた紙の上に色を置く技法です。乾いていない色に水や別の色をたらす方法もあり、にじみ効果が得られます。保水力のある紙にすると、にじみの伸びや広がりが得られます。
■Wet-on-wet
With this technique color is applied onto a wet paper. There are also ways of putting water and/or other colors onto a non-dry color to create effects of color-bleeding. If the paper has water holding capacities, it is also possible to spread and/or extend the bleeding.

■グラデーション
　ウォッシュの際に途中から絵の具の色を変えたり薄めたりすることでグラデーション（諧調表現）が得られます。保水力の高い紙ほど綺麗なグラデーションが作れます。
■Gradation
Gradation (tone expression) can be obtained by changing or diluting the color of the paint in the process of washing. Gradation can be made even more beautiful if the paper has high water holding capacities.

■拭き取り
　塗った色が完全に乾かないうちにティッシュや海綿などで軽く表面を当てて色を抜く技法です。別名リフティングとも言います。
■Lift-out
This technique is achieved by pressing tissue paper onto the surface of the painting or using a sponge to remove color before the paint is completely dry. It is also known as lifting.

■自由な表現法

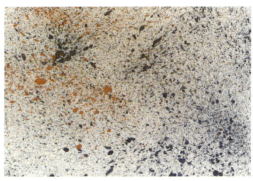

■ドリッピング
　太めの筆に絵の具をたっぷり含ませて、紙の上から絵の具をポタポタとたらす技法です。紙の質を選ばず描くことができます。
■*Splashing*
A technique where paint is dripped onto the paper from a thick brush containing a lot of paint. The quality of the paper is irrelevant with this technique

■スパッタリング
　筆を手や網で、はじいて絵の具を斑点状（はんてん）に散らして描く技法です。ドリッピングと同じく紙の質を選ばず描くことができます。
■*Sputtering*
Paint is spread over the paper in a spot-like/granular fashion, by flicking brushes or toothbrushes. Similar to splashing, the quality of the paper does not matter with this technique.

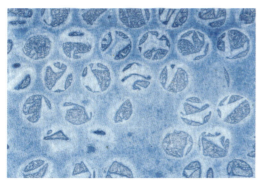

■エアパッキング　Bubble wrapping　　　　　　　　　■サランラップ　Saran wrapping
　絵の具を画面に塗ったあと、表面が乾かないうちにいろいろな素材を押し当てて偶然のマチエールを楽しむ技法です。吸水性のないエアパッキングやサランラップ、アルミホイルなど畳んだり丸めたりできるものを選びます。絵の具が乾きかけた頃に素材を取り除くとはっきりした模様が残ります。
This technique allows you to have fun by pressing various materials against the painting before the surface has dried. Choose a bubble wrap, saran wrap, aluminium foil etc. that can be folded or rolled and does not absorb the paint. When the paint is about to dry and the materials are removed, clear, distinct patterns are created.

■マスキング（ポジ・ネガ）
　白く抜きたい部分をあらかじめマスキング液かマスキングテープで保護してから色を塗る技法です。
　※マスキングテープは、絵具をかけたくない部分にあらかじめ貼っておくために作られたものです。
　※マスキング液は液体状で絵の具をつけたくない部分にあらかじめ筆やツケペンで塗っておくものです。
　表面強度の高い紙を使用する必要があります。
■*Masking (positive/negative)*
Using this technique allows you to protect the areas you want to keep from getting painted by applying color with a masking fluid or masking tape before painting.
※ Masking tape: will be taped to the part you do not want to apply paint before painting
※Masking fluid: will be applied with a brush or pen to the part you do not want to paint before painting

作：つちやきよこ　　*Written by: Kiyoko Tsuchiya*

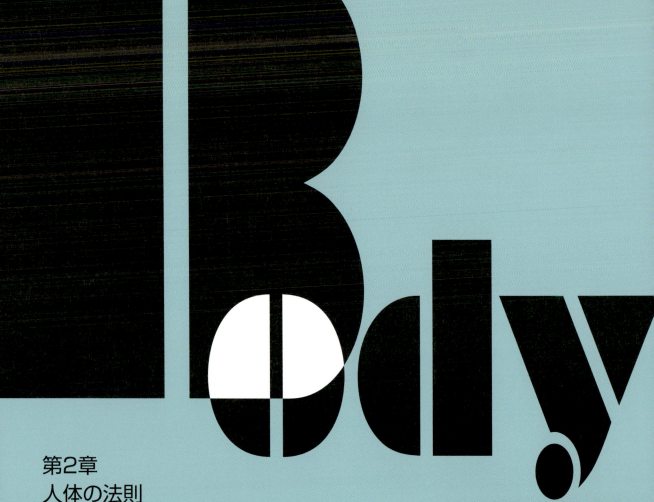

第2章
人体の法則

バランスの取れたプロポーションを描くことは
必ず身に付けておきたい基本的なスキルです。
ときには決められたルールや枠を打ち破り新境地を
開拓する…それがファッションの醍醐味でもあり
デザイナーのスピリッツでもありますが
最終的には服は人間が着てはじめて成り立ちます。
頭の中にあるアイデアを自由に描くためにも
人体の構造とプロポーションをしっかりと
理解しておくことが必要です。
発想を支える基礎を固め、基本のルールである
人体の法則を習得しましょう。

Chapter 2
Body Code (Body Construction)

To draw balanced proportions is one of basic skill
that you should acquire in the fashion design.
Such as breaking down the rules and frames that have
been decided and breaking new ground are the both
the best part of fashion and the spirit of designer.
However, clothes are able to exist only by being worn
by humans eventually. It is necessary to understand
the structure and proportions of the human body
well in order to freely draw ideas in your mind.
Let's solidify the basics to support the idea and acquire
the Body Code (Body Construction) that is basic rules.

■Body Code

人体のプロポーション The Proportions of Human body

　プロポーション（比例）とは、基準と全体との関係をいいます。
　人体のプロポーションを測るには頭部の長さを基準にするのが一般的です。人間のプロポーションは通常7.5頭身位ですがファッションの世界では服を引き立たせるために理想的プロポーションとして8.5頭身か9頭身、それ以上に描く場合もあります。

Proportion (proportional) refers to comparative relation between the base part and the whole as to size. It is common to use height of a head as a base part, in order to measure the proportion of the human body. Standard proportion of human body is measured as 7.5 heads high in the real. However, they often be drawn as 8.5, 9 or more heads high in the fashion world, as ideal proportions to make clothes stand out.

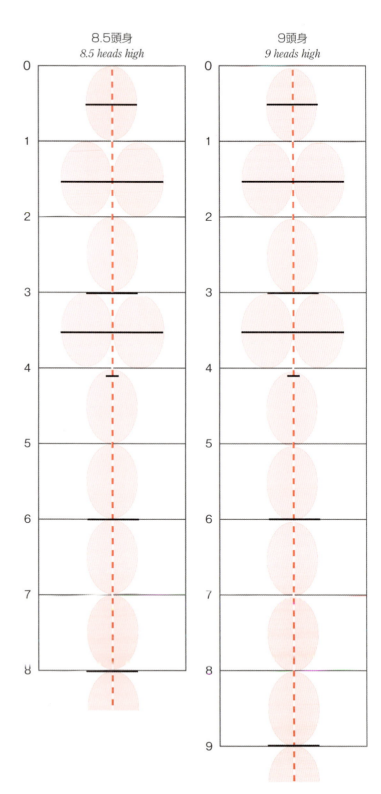

ウィトルウィウス的人体図
1487年ごろにレオナルド・ダ・ヴィンチが描いた世界的に有名な人体の黄金比。古代ローマ時代の建築家ウィトルウィウスの著作をもとに正確な人体のプロポーションを描き出しました。このドローイングは、「プロポーションの法則」、あるいは「人体の調和」と呼ばれることがあります。

The Vitruvian Man "The proportions of the human body according to Vitruvius", this is the world-famous drawing called "the golden ratio of human body" that was drawn by Leonardo da Vinci around 1487. He drew an accurate proportion of human body based on a piece of the ancient Roman architect Vitruvius. This drawing is sometimes called "the Canon of Proportions" or, less often, "Proportions of Man".

■ 人体の法則

頭部を基準に
肩幅とヒップは（頭部の幅）×2
ウエストは（頭部の幅）×1
*Use the head part as a base
Width of shoulder and hip is (width of the head part) × 2
Width of waist is (width of the head part) × 1*

9頭身で描く場合は膝から下を長く。
ボディや手のバランスは8.5頭身と全く同じバランス
When drawing with 9 heads high, extend the part under the knees while to keep the proportion of body and hands exactly same as 8.5 heads high.

8.5頭身　　　9頭身
8.5 heads high　*9 heads high*

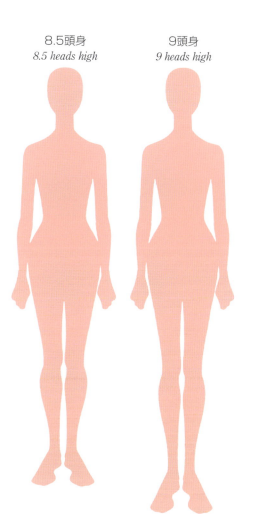

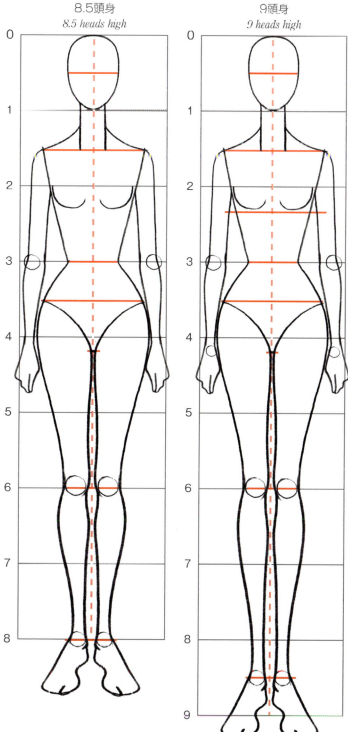

53

■Body Code

プロポーション（女性） *Proportion (Women)*

用紙のサイズに合わせてバランスよく8.5頭身のベースラインを引きます。
Drawing well-balanced baselines of 8.5 heads high according to the paper size.

  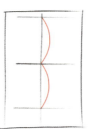 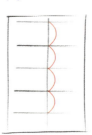  

❶縦に中心線を軽く引きます。
Drawing a vertical centerline lightly.

❷上から1cm、下から5〜6cmのところに横線を引きます。
Drawing two horizontal lines that are placed 1 cm from the top and 5〜6 cm from the bottom.

❸二等分した真ん中に横線を引きます。
Drawing a horizontal line that divides it in half.

❹二等分した間の等分のところに横線を引きます。
Drawing two horizontal lines that divide each divided space in half.

❺間の等分のところに横線を引き、上から番号を付けます。
Drawing four horizontal lines more that divide each divided space in half and putting numbers from the top.

❻9頭身の場合は下に一本線を付け足します。
In case of drawing 9 heads high, adding a line on the bottom.

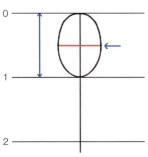 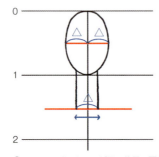 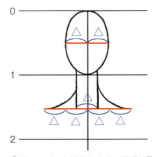

❶0〜1の間に顔。頭部の長さ2/3が横幅。
Placing a face in the space of 0〜1. The width of head is 2/3 of the length of head.

❷1〜2の1/2のところが肩の位置。頭部の横幅1/2が首幅。
Placing the shoulder position at 1/2 in 1〜2. The width of neck is 1/2 of the width of head.

❸肩のラインを補正します。肩幅は頭部の横幅×2。
Correcting the shoulder line. The width of shoulder is the width of the head × 2.

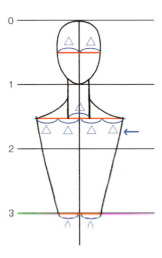 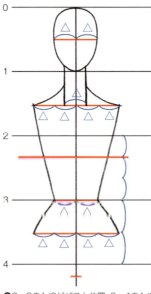 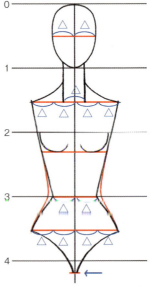

❹2の肩幅から3のウエスト位置をつなげます。ウエストは頭部の横幅。
Connecting the waist position of 3 from the shoulder width of 2. The width of waist is the same width of head.

❺2〜3の1/3がバスト位置、3〜4の1/2がヒップライン。ウエストからヒップラインをつなげます。
Connecting the hip line from the waist. Placing the bust position at 1/3 from the top of 2〜3. Placing the hip line at 1/2 in 3〜4.

❻4〜5の1/5が股上の位置。ヒップラインから股上の位置に足の付け根ラインを描きウエストを補正。
Placing the crotch position at 1/5 from the top of 4〜5. Drawing baselines of legs from hip line to crotch position and correcting the waist.

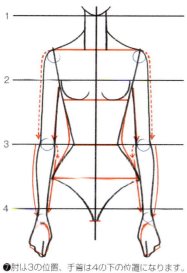

腕は肩の丸みを出しながら3の肘の位置まで真っすぐ。
Drawing the arm straight down to the position of the elbow on 3 while expressing the roundness of shoulders.

肘から手首に向かって内側は真っすぐ、外側はカーブをつけます。
Drawing straight line from the elbow to the wrist for inner side, and drawing a curved line for outer side.

手は半楕円の形に描きます。
Drawing a hand in semi-elliptical shape.

❼肘は3の位置、手首は4の下の位置になります。
Placing the elbow at the position 3 and placing the wrist under the position 4.

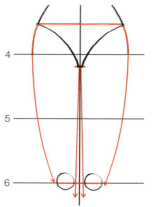

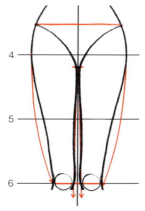

❽ヒップラインから6の位置まで内側は直線で、外側は大きく丸みを帯びるように軽く当たりをつけておきます。
Giving a rough guide from the hip line to the position 6 by straight line for inner side and big curved line for outer side.

❾4～5の間の外側は丸みを残し5～6の間は直線的に描き、内側は5～6の位置で直線より少し内側に描きます。
Drawing a curved line in 4~5 and a straight line in 5~6 for outer side. Drawing a slightly incurved line in 5~6 for inner side.

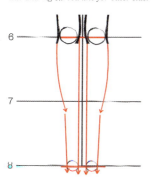

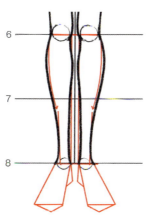

❿6～8まで内側は真っすぐに外側は6～7まで曲線、7～8は真っすぐに当たりをつけます。
Giving a rough guide for inner side with a straight line in 6~8, and giving a rough guide for outer side with a curved line in 6~7 and a straight line in 7~8.

⓫足は台形の形に描き踵とつま先部分は三角の形に当たりをつけます。
Giving a rough guide of trapezoidal shapes for the feet and adding triangular shapes on the heels and toes.

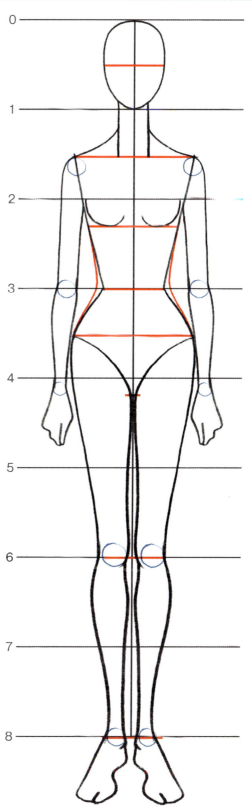

⓬最後に全体のバランスを整えて仕上げます。
Finishing by correcting the whole balance at the end.

■Body Code

プロポーション（男性） *Proportion (Men)*

用紙のサイズに合わせてバランスよく8.5頭身のベースラインを引きます。
Drawing well-balanced baselines of 8.5 heads high according to the paper size.

   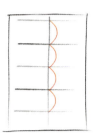  

❶縦に中心線を軽く引きます。
Drawing a vertical centerline lightly.

❷上から1cm、下から5〜6cmのところに横線を引きます。
Drawing two horizontal lines that are placed 1 cm from the top and 5〜6 cm from the bottom.

❸二等分した真ん中に横線を引きます。
Drawing a horizontal line that divides it in half.

❹二等分した間の等分のところに横線を引きます。
Drawing two horizontal lines that divide each divided space in half.

❺間の等分のところに横線を引き、上から番号を付けます。
Drawing four horizontal lines more that divide each divided space in half and putting numbers from the top.

❻9頭身の場合は下に一本線を付け足します。
In case of drawing 9 heads high, adding a line on the bottom.

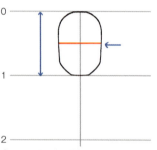 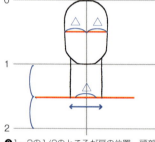 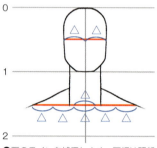

❶0〜1の間に顔。頭部の長さ2/3が横幅。
Placing a face in the space of 0〜1. The width of head is 2/3 of the length of head.

❷1〜2の1/2のところが肩の位置。頭部の横幅1/2が首幅。
Placing the shoulder position at 1/2 in 1〜2. The width of neck is 1/2 of the width of head.

❸肩のラインを補正します。肩幅は頭部の横幅1/2×5。
Correcting the shoulder line. The width of shoulder is 1/2 of the head width × 5.

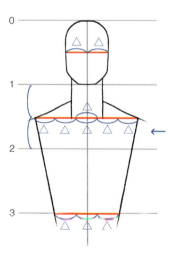 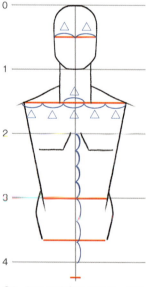 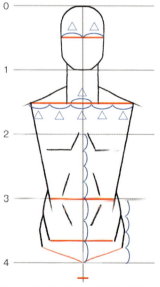

❹2の肩幅から3のウエスト位置をつなげます。ウエストは頭部1/2×3。
Connecting the waist position of 3 from the shoulder width position of 2. The width of waist is 1/2 of the head width × 3.

❺2〜3の1/4がバスト位置。3〜4の2/3がウエストの筋肉位置。ウエストの筋肉位置を確認します。
Placing the bust position at 1/4 from the top of 2〜3. Placing the muscle position of waist at 2/3 from the top of 3〜4. Confirming the muscle position of waist.

❻ヒップラインから股上の位置に足の付け根ラインを描きます。3〜4の3/4がヒップライン。
Drawing the leg baselines from hip line to crotch position. Placing the hip line at 3/4 from the top of 3〜4.

56

■人体の法則

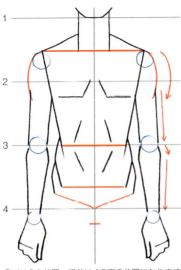

腕は肩の丸みを出しながら3の肘の位置まで真っすぐ。
Drawing the arm straight down to the position of the elbow on 3 while expressing the roundness of shoulders.

肘から手首に向かって内側は真っすぐ、外側はカーブをつけます。
Drawing straight line from the elbow to the wrist for inner side, and drawing a curved line for outer side.

手は半楕円の形に描きます。
Drawing a hand in semi-elliptical shape.

❼肘は3の位置、手首は4の下の位置になります。
Placing the elbow at the position 3 and placing the wrist under the position 4.

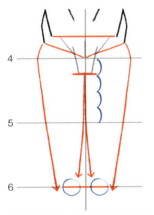

❽足の付け根から6の位置まで内側は直線で、外側は大きく丸みを帯びるように当たりをつけます。4～5の1/4が股上の位置。
Giving a rough guide from the base of legs to the position of 6 by a straight line for inner side and big curved line for outer side. Placing the crotch position at 1/4 from the top of 4-5.

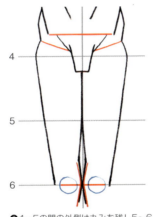

❾4～5の間の外側は丸みを残し5～6の間は直線的に描き、内側は5～6の位置で直線より少し内側に描きます。
Drawing a curved line in 4~5 and a straight line in 5-6 for outer side. Drawing a slightly incurved line in 5~6 for inner side.

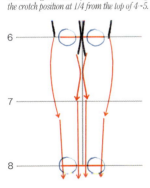

❿6～8まで内側は真っすぐに外側は6～7まで曲線、7～8は真っすぐに当たりをつけます。
Giving a rough guide for inner side with a straight line in 6~8, and giving a rough guide for outer side with a curved line in 6~7 and a straight line in 7~8.

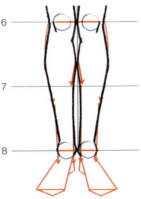

⓫足は台形の形に描き踵とつま先部分は三角の形に当たりをつけます。
Giving a rough guide of trapezoidal shapes for the feet and adding triangular shapes on the heels and toes.

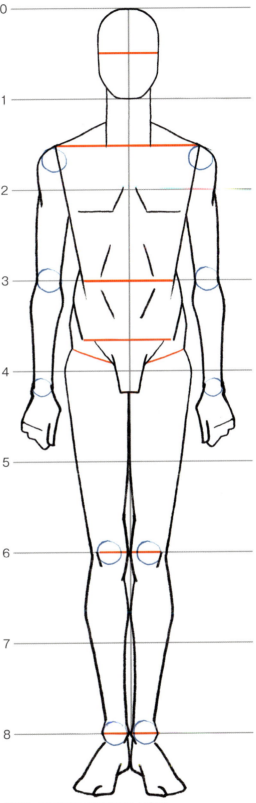

⓬最後に全体のバランスを整えて仕上げます。
Finishing by correcting the whole balance at the end.

57

正面片足重心ポーズ（女性）Front pose with center of gravity on one-foot (Women)

重心とは身体の重みや力を支えている点のことですが、人は緊張を解いてリラックスしている時に自然と片足に体重をかけた姿勢になります。片足に体重移動した時に体重がかかった方の腰は上がり、肩は下がります。重心がどこにあり、どこでバランスをとっているかが大切です。

The center of gravity is the point that supports the weight of the body. People put their weight on one-foot naturally when they release the tension and relax. When people put their weight on one-foot, they raise the waist that is on weight-bearing side and down the shoulder on the same side. It is important to understand where is the part that people have center of gravity and where is the point that people are balancing.

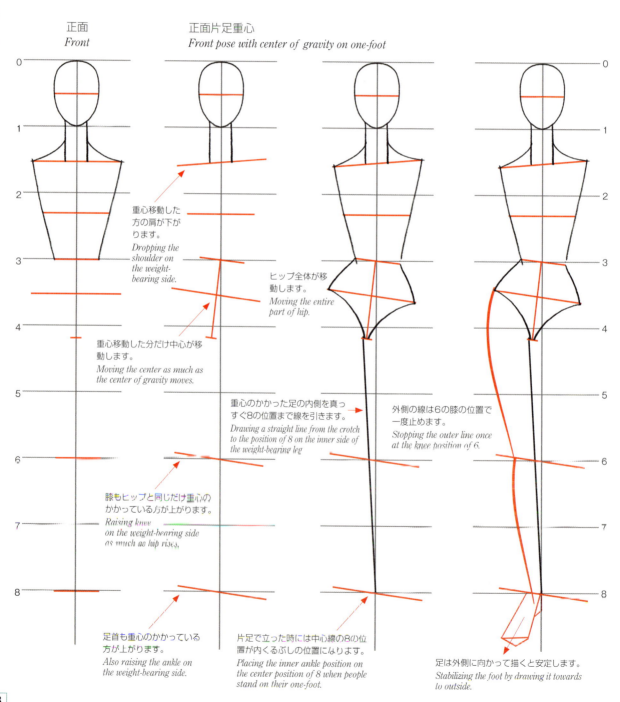

■ 人体の法則

肩が下がると腰が上がります
Raising the waist when the shoulder drops.

体重がかかっている脚のくるぶしが中心線に戻り来す
Bringing back the ankle on the weight-bearing side to the centerline.

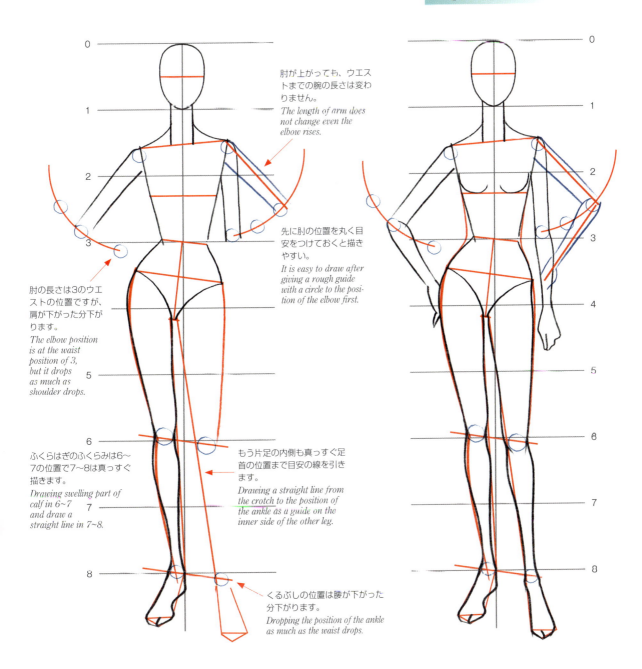

肘が上がっても、ウエストまでの腕の長さは変わりません。
The length of arm does not change even the elbow rises.

先に肘の位置を丸く目安をつけておくと描きやすい。
It is easy to draw after giving a rough guide with a circle to the position of the elbow first.

肘の長さは3のウエストの位置ですが、肩が下がった分下がります。
The elbow position is at the waist position of 3, but it drops as much as shoulder drops.

ふくらはぎのふくらみは6〜7の位置で7〜8は真っすぐ描きます。
Drawing swelling part of calf in 6~7 and draw a straight line in 7~8.

もう片足の内側も真っすぐ足首の位置まで目安の線を引きます。
Drawing a straight line from the crotch to the position of the ankle as a guide on the inner side of the other leg.

くるぶしの位置は腰が下がった分下がります。
Dropping the position of the ankle as much as the waist drops.

59

■Body Code

正面片足重心ポーズ（男性） Front pose with center of gravity on one-foot (Men)

男性も女性と同じく肩、腰の位置や重心がどこにあり、どこでバランスをとっているかが大切です。
It is important to understand where is the shoulder, the waist, the part that people have center of gravity and where is the point that people are balancing, as same as the posing of women.

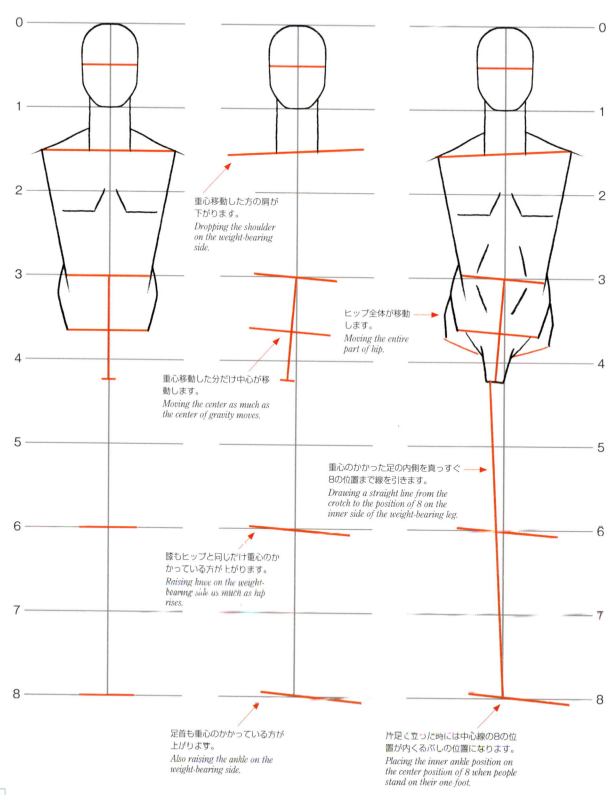

重心移動した方の肩が下がります。
Dropping the shoulder on the weight-bearing side.

重心移動した分だけ中心が移動します。
Moving the center as much as the center of gravity moves.

ヒップ全体が移動します。
Moving the entire part of hip.

重心のかかった足の内側を真っすぐ8の位置まで線を引きます。
Drawing a straight line from the crotch to the position of 8 on the inner side of the weight-bearing leg.

膝もヒップと同じだけ重心のかかっている方が上がります。
Raising knee on the weight-bearing side as much as hip rises.

足首も重心のかかっている方が上がります。
Also raising the ankle on the weight-bearing side.

片足で立った時には中心線の8の位置が内くるぶしの位置になります。
Placing the inner ankle position on the center position of 8 when people stand on their one foot.

60

■ 人体の法則

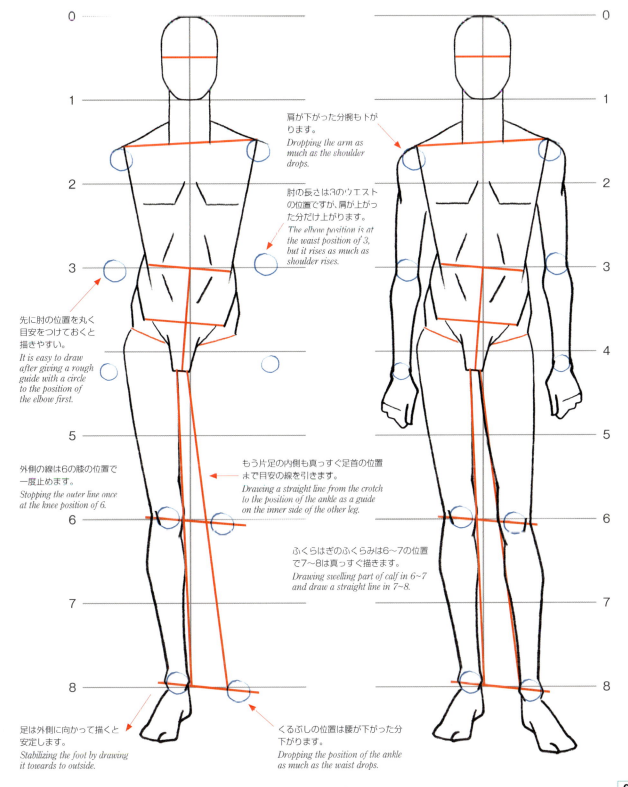

■Body Code

斜め片足重心ポーズ（女性） Angled pose with center of gravity on one-foot (Women)

　身体全体が斜めを向くと中心は大きく移動します。どちらの足で身体を支えているかで肩や腰も大きく動きますが、身体を支える軸足の内くるぶしが必ず身体の中心に戻るという法則をふまえることで、安定したバランスをとることができます。

The centerline of the body moves a lot as well as the shoulders and hip depending on which foot supports the body, when the entire body turns diagonally. It is easy to make a stable pose with good balance if you draw it based on the body law that the inner ankle of the weight-bearing leg always returns to the center of the body.

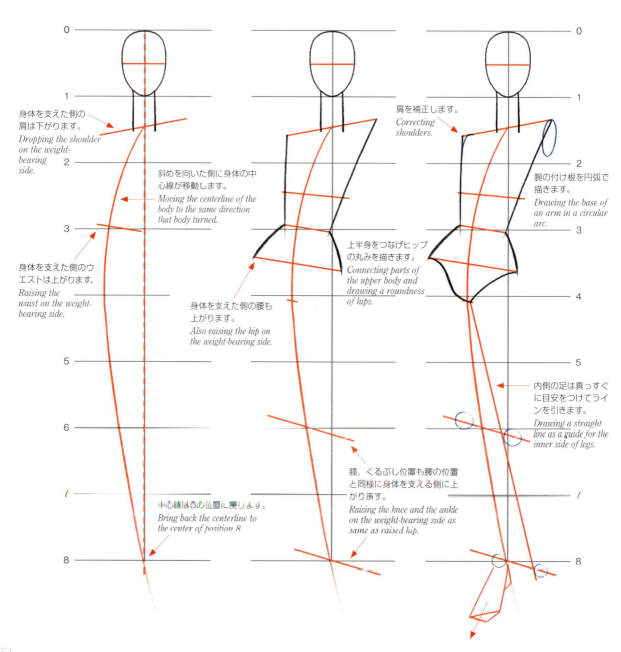

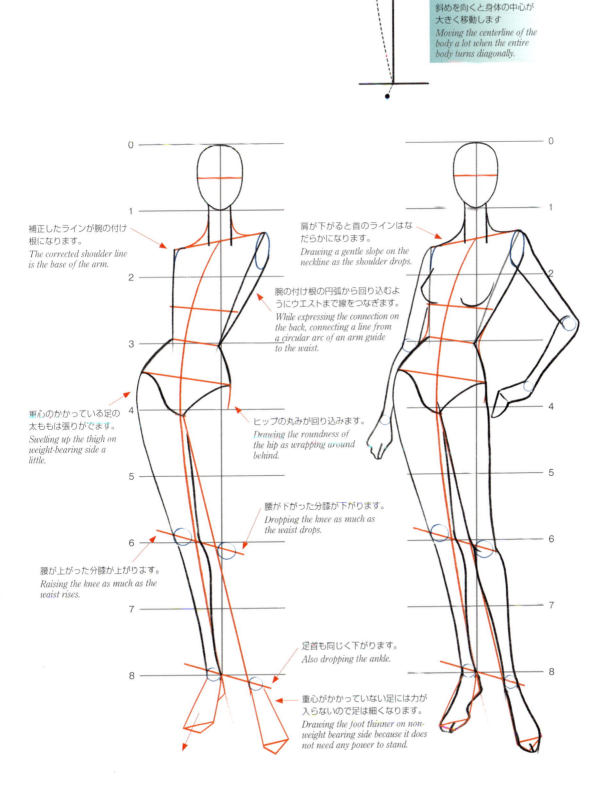

斜め片足重心ポーズ（男性） *Angled pose with center of gravity on one-foot (Men)*

　男性も女性と同じく身体を支える軸足の内くるぶしが、必ず身体の中心に戻るという法則をふまえることで、安定したバランスをとることができます。
It is easy to make a stable pose with good balance if you draw it based on the body law that the inner ankle of the weight-bearing leg always returns to the center of the body, as same as the posing of women.

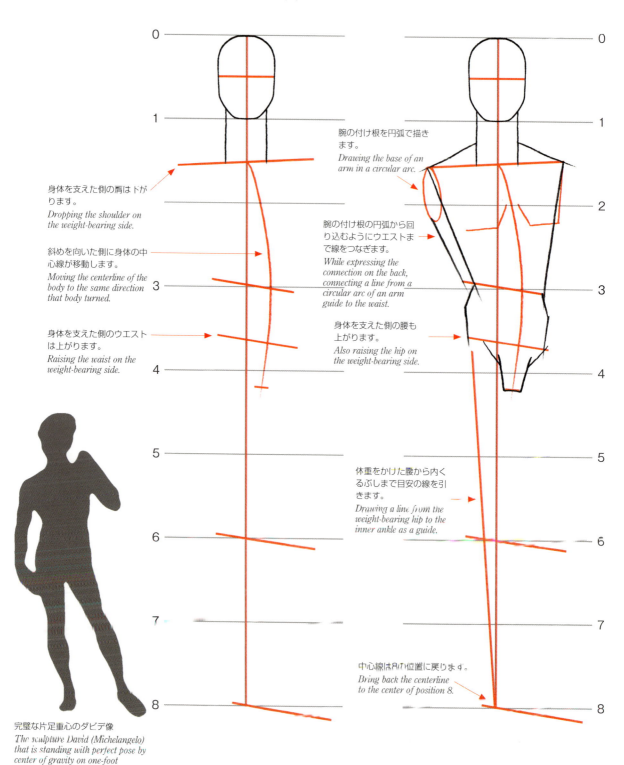

身体を支えた側の肩は下がります。
Dropping the shoulder on the weight-bearing side.

斜めを向いた側に身体の中心線が移動します。
Moving the centerline of the body to the same direction that body turned.

身体を支えた側のウエストは上がります。
Raising the waist on the weight-bearing side.

腕の付け根を円弧で描きます。
Drawing the base of an arm in a circular arc.

腕の付け根の円弧から回り込むようにウエストまで線をつなぎます。
While expressing the connection on the back, connecting a line from a circular arc of an arm guide to the waist.

身体を支えた側の腰も上がります。
Also raising the hip on the weight-bearing side.

体重をかけた腰から内くるぶしまで目安の線を引きます。
Drawing a line from the weight-bearing hip to the inner ankle as a guide.

中心線は8の位置に戻ります。
Bring back the centerline to the center of position 8.

完璧な片足重心のダビデ像
The sculpture David (Michelangelo) that is standing with perfect pose by center of gravity on one-foot

■人体の法則

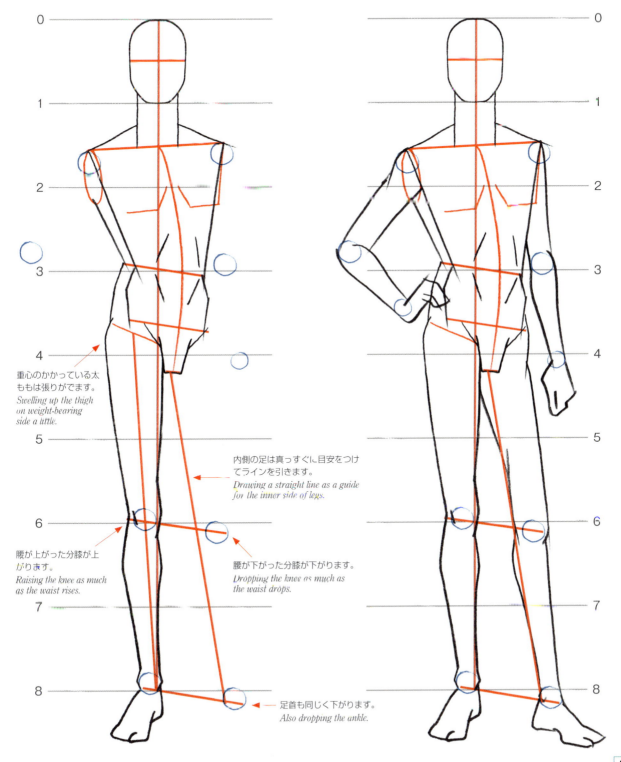

重心のかかっている太
ももは張りがでます。
*Swelling up the thigh
on weight-bearing
side a little.*

内側の足は真っすぐに目安をつけ
てラインを引きます。
*Drawing a straight line as a guide
for the inner side of legs.*

腰が上がった分膝が上
がります。
*Raising the knee as much
as the waist rises.*

腰が下がった分膝が下がります。
*Dropping the knee as much as
the waist drops.*

足首も同じく下がります。
Also dropping the ankle.

65

■Body Code

後ろ・横ポーズ（女性／男性） *Back・Profile (Side) pose (Women/Men)*

　後ろポーズは正面ポーズと同じバランスですが、首、ヒップ、手と足の向きに注意しながら描きます。横ポーズは胸が中心より前に、腰から下は重心が後ろにかかり気味にS字ラインのように描きます。

The back pose is the same balance as the front pose, but draw it while paying attention to the directions of neck, hip, hand and foot. For the profile (side) pose, the bust towards the front side than the centerline, the center of gravity for waist and its lower goes to the back a little, and it is drawn as an S-shaped line.

（女性）
(Women)

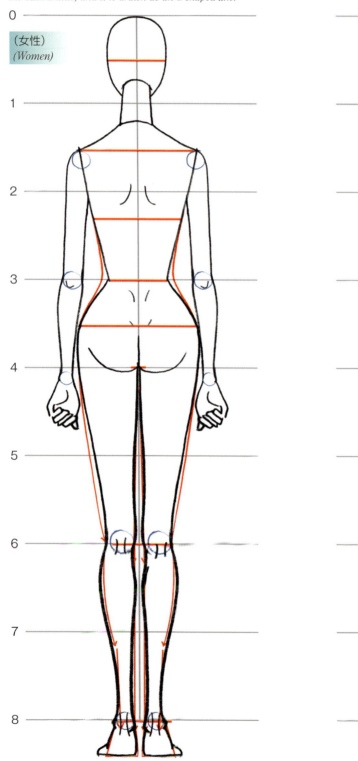
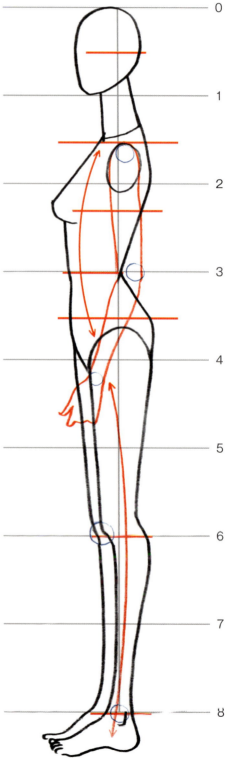

■人体の法則

（男性）
(Men)

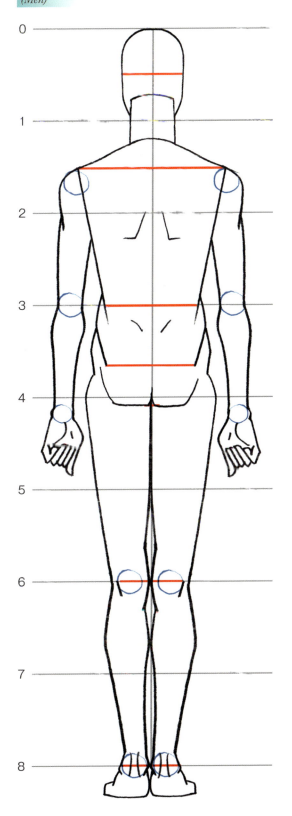
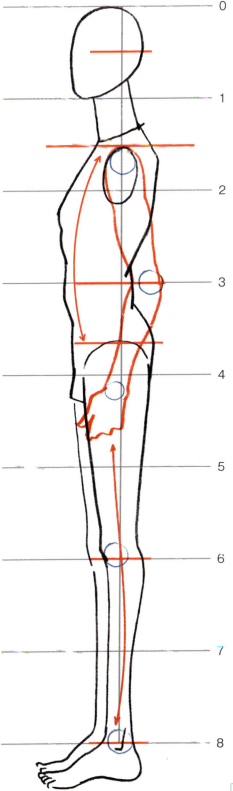

■Body Code

顔を描く *Drawing a face*

左右対称で複雑なパーツを持つ顔ですが、単純な図形に置き換えて位置を確認しながら描くと、バランスがとりやすくなります。
A face has symmetrical and complex parts, but it is easy to have a good balance if you draw it with replacing simple figures while checking its position.

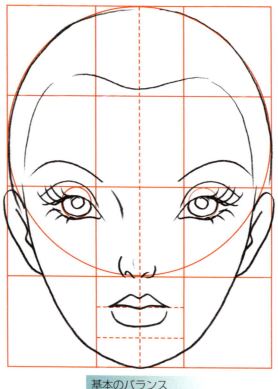

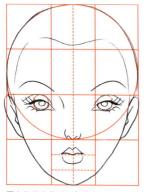

逆三角形のバランス
Inverted triangle balance

目とあごのラインを細くして口を小さく描きます。
Drawing a small mouth with making the eyes and chin thinner.

基本のバランス
Basic balance

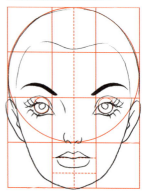

四角形のバランス
Square balance

目を大きく、あごのラインを張り気味に口を大きく描きます。
Drawing eyes and a mouth bigger, and making the chin line wider a little.

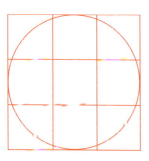 → 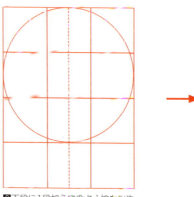 →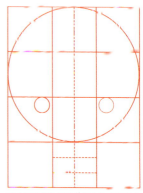

①正方形の縦と横を3等分し大きな円を描きます。
Dividing the square into three equal parts vertically and horizontally, and drawing a big circle.

②下段に1段加え縦の中心線を引きます。
Adding a column to the bottom and drawing a vertical centerline.

③1/2下段に目の位置を取り下段の正方形を3等分します。
Putting the position of eyes just under the 1/2 line and dividing the bottom center square into three equal parts horizontally.

68

■ 人体の法則

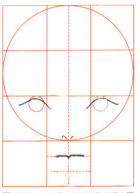 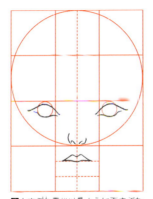 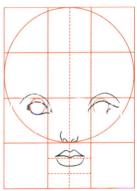

4 3等分した上段に口の中心を描き下段の正方形の真上に鼻先を描きます。
Drawing the center of the mouth in the upper part of the trisection and drawing the tip of the nose just above the bottom center square.

5 上まぶたを受けるように下まぶたを描き、上唇と鼻を描き加えます。
Drawing a bottom eyelid as receiving the top eyelid, and drawing an upper lip and a nose.

6 上まぶたの上に二重の線を加えます。下唇は上唇より厚めに描きます。
Adding a double line over the upper eyelid and drawing the lower lip thicker than the upper lip.

 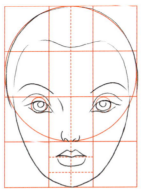 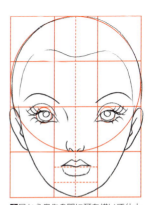

7 円に沿って頭の輪郭を描き耳の厚み分を残して顔の輪郭を描きます。
Drawing a contour of the head along the circle and drawing a contour of the face while leaving a thickness of the ears.

8 瞳を描き加えてまつげを描きます。眉毛は眉尻を上げるように描くと引き締まります。
Drawing eyelashes and adding eyes. The eyebrows can be tightened with drawing as raising the end of eyebrow.

9 目から鼻先の間に耳を描いて仕上げます。
Finishing by drawing ears in the position between eyes and the tip of the nose.

上を向いた顔
Face looking up

正面
Front

下を向いた顔
Face looking down

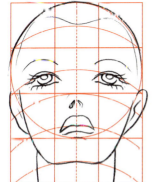 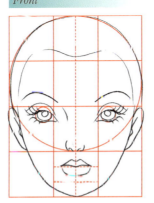 

▲ 上を向くとあごが上がり目尻、眉、口角が下がって見えます。上唇が厚く下唇が薄く見え首も太くなります。
When the face up, the jaws rise and the end of eyes, eyebrows and the corners of the mouth drops. The upper lip and the neck become thicker at the same time the lower lip becomes thinner.

▼ 下を向くと目尻、眉、口角が上がって見え耳も上がり、上唇が薄く下唇が厚く見えます。
When the face down, the end of eyes, eyebrows, and the corners of the mouth rise as well as ears. Upper lip becomes thinner and lower lip becomes thicker.

69

■Body Code

いろいろな角度の顔　Faces of various angles

　角度によって変化する顔を描くのは難しいのですが、一定の法則を理解すると格段に描きやすくなります。例えば上を向くと眉、目尻、耳、口角が下がって見え鼻の穴も大きく見えてきます。逆に下を向くと眉、目尻、耳、口角が上がって見えるのです。

Although it is difficult to draw a face that changes depending on various angles, it is easy to draw if you understand certain laws. For example, dropping the eyebrows, the end of eyes, the ears and corners of the mouth, and showing the holes in the nose larger, when you draw the looking up face. On the other hand, raising all those elements when you draw the looking down face.

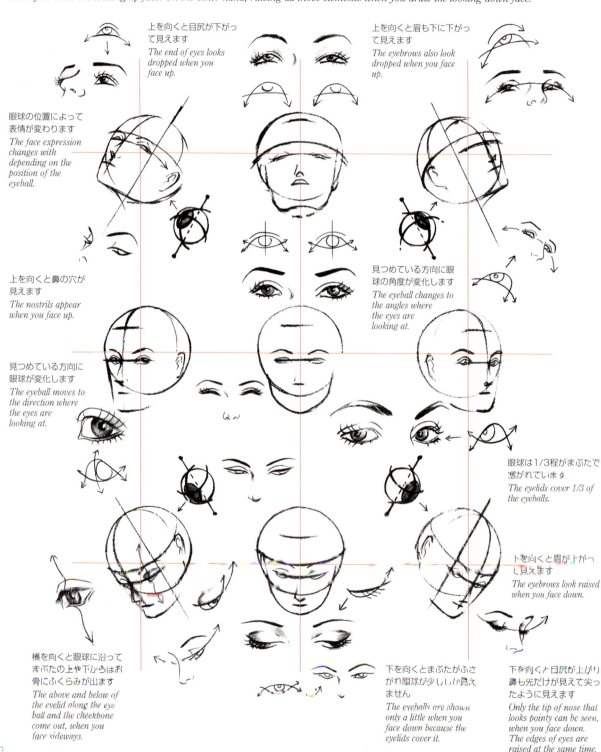

上を向くと目尻が下がって見えます
The end of eyes looks dropped when you face up.

上を向くと眉も下に下がって見えます
The eyebrows also look dropped when you face up.

眼球の位置によって表情が変わります
The face expression changes with depending on the position of the eyeball.

見つめている方向に眼球の角度が変化します
The eyeball changes to the angles where the eyes are looking at.

上を向くと鼻の穴が見えます
The nostrils appear when you face up.

見つめている方向に眼球が変化します
The eyeball moves to the direction where the eyes are looking at.

眼球は1/3程がまぶたで覆われています
The eyelids cover 1/3 of the eyeballs.

下を向くと眉が上がって見えます
The eyebrows look raised when you face down.

横を向くと眼球に沿ってまぶたの上や下からほお骨にふくらみが出ます
The above and below of the eyelid along the eyeball and the cheekbone come out, when you face sideways.

下を向くとまぶたがふさがれ眼球が少ししか見えません
The eyeballs are shown only a little when you face down because the eyelids cover it.

下を向くと目尻が上がり鼻も先だけが見えて尖ったように見えます
Only the tip of nose that looks pointy can be seen, when you face down. The edges of eyes are raised at the same time.

70

唇の描き方 How to draw a lip

1 口の大きさに線を引いて中心に印をつけておきます。
Drawing a line of the size for the mouth and putting a guide mark on the center.

2 唇の厚さに合わせて目安の○を上に二つ、下に二つ描き足します。
Drawing a guide circle of three on the top and two on the bottom according to the thickness of the lips.

3 口角から○を囲むように描き中心の○に段差を付けます。
Drawing an outline around those circles from the corner of mouth and putting a small gap on the center circle.

4 モデルのイメージや表情に合わせて修正し仕上げます。
Finishing by correcting it according to the image and face expression of models.

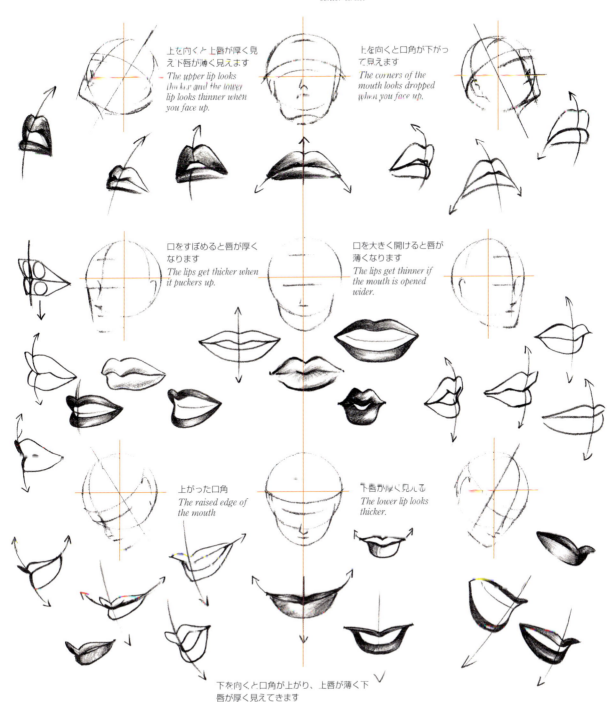

上を向くと上唇が厚く見え下唇が薄く見えます
The upper lip looks thicker and the lower lip looks thinner when you face up.

上を向くと口角が下がって見えます
The corners of the mouth looks dropped when you face up.

口をすぼめると唇が厚くなります
The lips get thicker when it puckers up.

口を大きく開けると唇が薄くなります
The lips get thinner if the mouth is opened wider.

上がった口角
The raised edge of the mouth

下唇が厚く見えます
The lower lip looks thicker.

下を向くと口角が上がり、上唇が薄く下唇が厚く見えてきます
The edges of the mouth rise when you face down. At the same time, the upper lip looks thinner and the lower lip looks thicker.

■Body Code

帽子を描く *Drawing a hat*

帽子を描くときは、必ず頭の輪郭を確認することが大切です。かぶりの位置が深いときには頭部の深さが足りなくなったり、ブリムの大きい場合は頭の輪郭より小さくなってしまうことがあります

It is important to check the contour of the head when you draw a hat. The length of head may become shorten when it wears the hat deeply and the outline of head may get smaller when it wears hat with big brim.

ブリム（帽子の縁）
Brim (the projecting edge around the bottom of a hat)

クラウン（帽子の山）
Crown (the top part of hat)

眼球の位置によって表情が変わります
Drawing the silhouette of hat with checking the contour of the head.

■人体の法則

73

■Body Code

手を描く *Drawing a hand*

複雑な動きをする手を描くことは難しく感じますが、シンプルなフォルムに置き換えることで単純な動きから表情のある動きまで自由に描くことができます。

Although it seems difficult to draw hands that move complicated, it is possible to draw various movements from simple to expressive one easily, by replacing them with simple shapes.

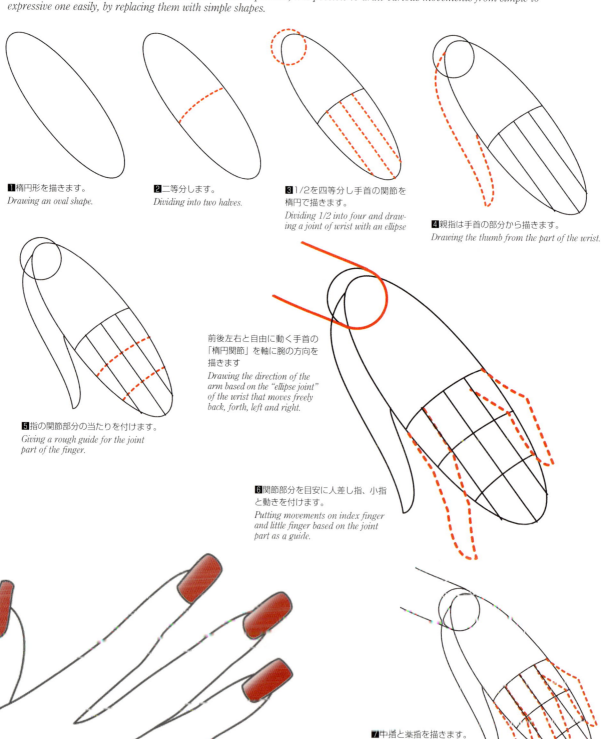

■1 楕円形を描きます。
Drawing an oval shape.

■2 二等分します。
Dividing into two halves.

■3 1/2を四等分し手首の関節を楕円で描きます。
Dividing 1/2 into four and drawing a joint of wrist with an ellipse

■4 親指は手首の部分から描きます。
Drawing the thumb from the part of the wrist.

■5 指の関節部分の当たりを付けます。
Giving a rough guide for the joint part of the finger.

前後左右と自由に動く手首の「楕円関節」を軸に腕の方向を描きます
Drawing the direction of the arm based on the "ellipse joint" of the wrist that moves freely back, forth, left and right.

■6 関節部分を目安に人差し指、小指と動きを付けます。
Putting movements on index finger and little finger based on the joint part as a guide.

■7 中指と薬指を描きます。
Draw the middle finger and ring finger

74

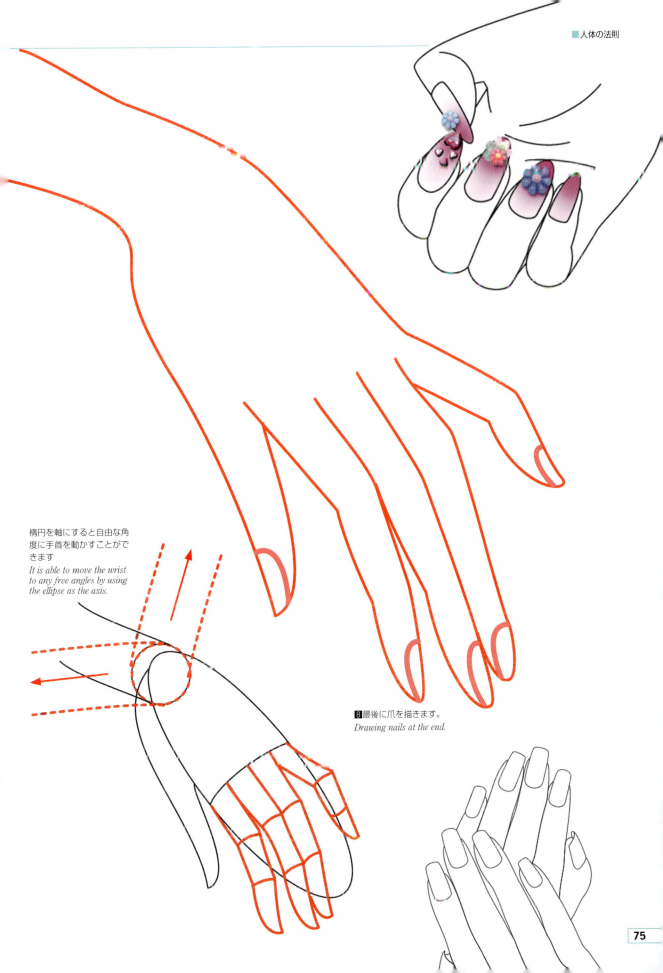

■人体の法則

楕円を軸にすると自由な角度に手首を動かすことができます
It is able to move the wrist to any free angles by using the ellipse as the axis.

⑧最後に爪を描きます。
Drawing nails at the end.

75

いろいろな角度の手 Hands of various angles

横向きの手も最初に全体のフォルムを描き、あとから親指を描き加えます
Drawing the whole form of hands on lateral position first, and adding the thumb later.

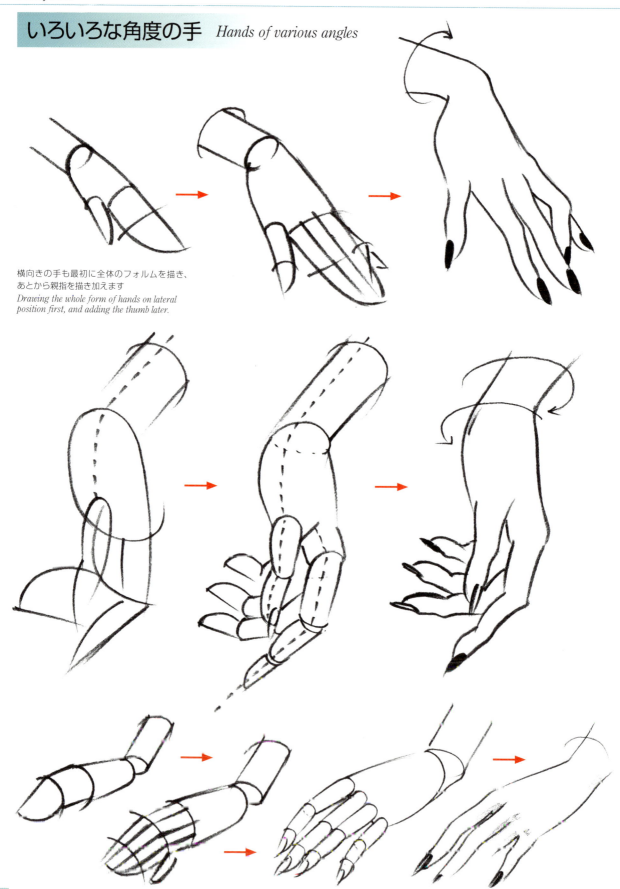

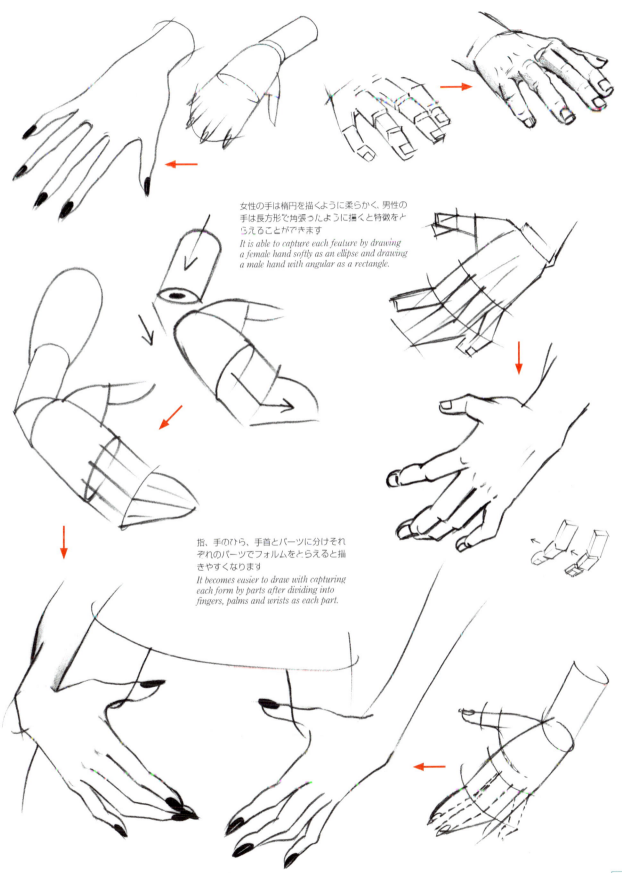

■人体の法則

女性の手は楕円を描くように柔らかく、男性の手は長方形で肩張ったように描くと特徴をとらえることができます
It is able to capture each feature by drawing a female hand softly as an ellipse and drawing a male hand with angular as a rectangle.

指、手のひら、手首とパーツに分けそれぞれのパーツでフォルムをとらえると描きやすくなります
It becomes easier to draw with capturing each form by parts after dividing into fingers, palms and wrists as each part.

77

■Body Code

手と手袋 *Hands and gloves*

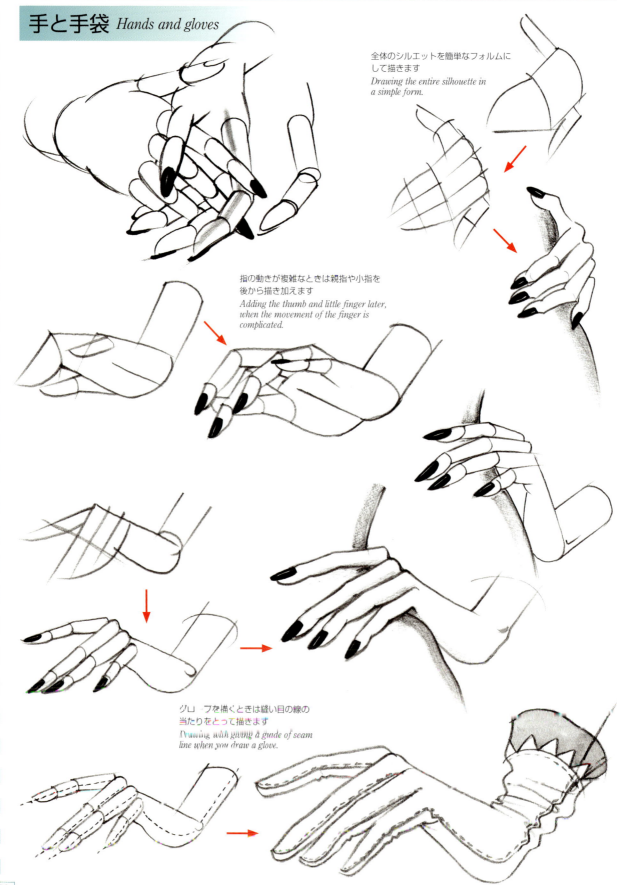

全体のシルエットを簡単なフォルムにして描きます
Drawing the entire silhouette in a simple form.

指の動きが複雑なときは親指や小指を後から描き加えます
Adding the thumb and little finger later, when the movement of the finger is complicated.

グローブを描くときは縫い目の線の当たりをとって描きます
Drawing with giving a guide of seam line when you draw a glove.

■ 人体の法則

手首や指など関節部分の曲がるところにシワがよります
Expressing the wrinkles at the bends of joint parts such as wrists and fingers.

①グローブを描くとき
②親指の付け根に
③切り替え線が入ります
Putting a seam line at the base of the thumb when you draw a glove

■Body Code

足を描く Drawing a foot

身体を支える足は、かかと、甲、そして指の部分とに分けて単純な図形におきかえてみると簡単に描けます。
It is easy to draw a foot by simple shapes with dividing into the heel, the instep and the finger part.

フラットな状態 State of flat

1 線を四等分し正方形を4つ描きます。
Dividing the line into four equal part and drawing 4 squares.

2 ①に指先、③に土踏まず、④にかかとを描きます。
Drawing a fingertip on (1), an arch of a foot on (3), and a heel on (4).

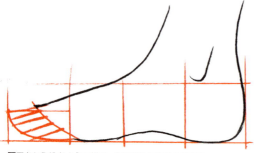

3 甲を包み込むように描き、指の当たり線を入れます。
Drawing the instep as to wrap around, and giving a rough guide of fingers.

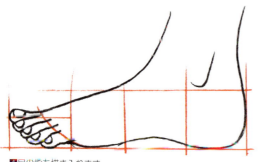

4 足の指を描き入れます。
Drawing the fingers in the foot.

かかとを上げた状態 State of the raised heel

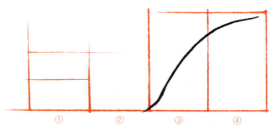

1 土踏まずは大きく傾斜をつけます。
Inclining the arch of a foot strongly.

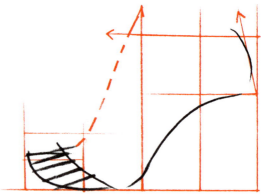

2 前に体重移動するためかかとも大きく前に傾斜します。
Inclining the heel strongly to the front as the weight shifts forward.

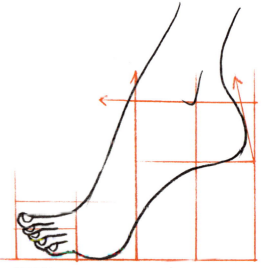

3 つま先部分に力がかかるために甲は伸びて大きく傾斜します。
Inclining and extending the instep strongly as the toe part is applied pressure.

■人体の法則

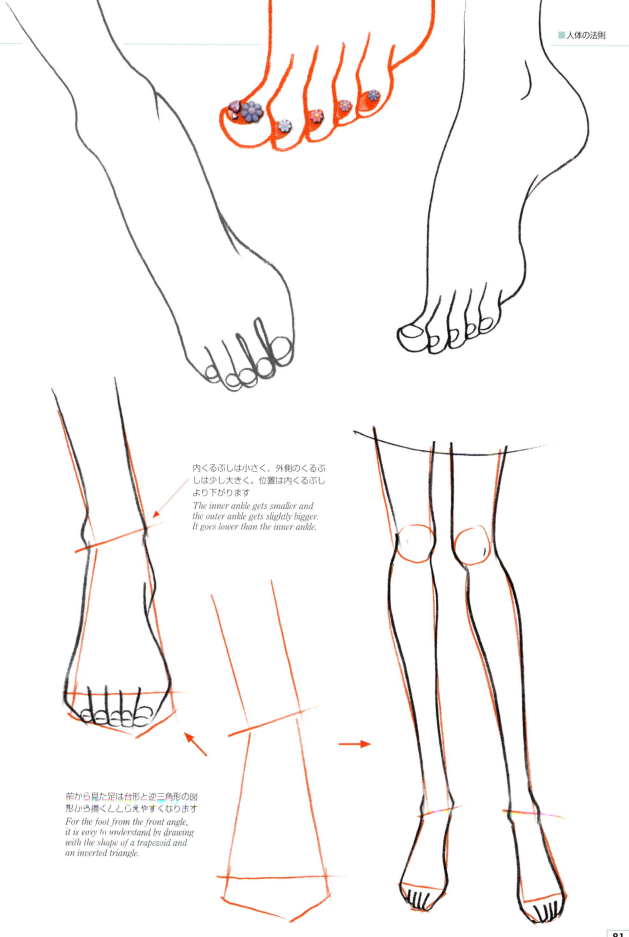

内くるぶしは小さく、外側のくるぶしは少し大きく。位置は内くるぶしより下がります
The inner ankle gets smaller and the outer ankle gets slightly bigger. It goes lower than the inner ankle.

前から見た足は台形と逆三角形の図形から描くととらえやすくなります
For the foot from the front angle, it is easy to understand by drawing with the shape of a trapezoid and an inverted triangle.

■Body Code

靴を描く／側面（ローヒール） Drawing shoes/low heel (Profile/Side)

造形的でフォルムがはっきりした靴は、かかと、甲、そして指の部分とに分けて単純な図形で描くと簡単に描けます。
It is easy to draw shoes that have formative clear form, by simple shapes with dividing into the heel, the instep and the finger part.

■1 横に線を真っすぐ引き四等分して印をつけます。
Drawing a straight horizontal line and dividing it into four equal parts while putting marks.

■2 1/4の部分がヒールになります。
The part of 1/4 is a heel.

■3 1/4～2/4部分に土踏まずのカーブを描き、つま先部分を浮かせて繋ぐと底部分になります。
Drawing a curve for an arch of a foot at 1/4~2/4 part, and connecting the lines to make it as a sole while leaving the toe part raising.

下から上に立ち上がるように描きます。
Drawing it as standing up from the bottom to the top.

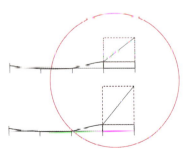

かかと部分の正方形を短くしたり長くするとシルエットが変わります。
The silhouette changes depending on the square of the heel part changes shorter or longer.

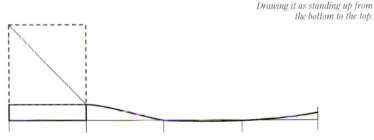

■4 かかと部分は1/4のヒール部分から正方形を描きます。
Drawing a square for the heel part on the 1/4 part of the line.

82

■ 人体の法則

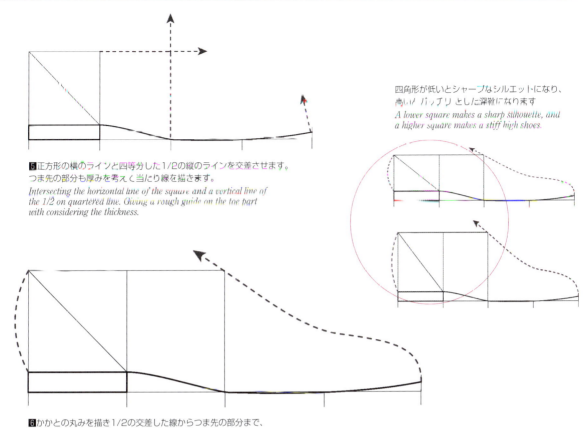

四角形が低いとシャープなシルエットになり、高いとバッチリとした深靴になります
A lower square makes a sharp silhouette, and a higher square makes a stiff high shoes.

5 正方形の横のラインと四等分した1/2の縦のラインを交差させます。つま先の部分も厚みを考えて当たり線を描きます。
Intersecting the horizontal line of the square and a vertical line of the 1/2 on quartered line. Giving a rough guide on the toe part with considering the thickness.

6 かかとの丸みを描き1/2の交差した線からつま先の部分まで、甲を包み込むようにつなげて描きます。
Drawing the heel with roundness and drawing the line from 1/2 crossing line to the toe part as to wrap around the instep.

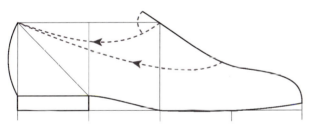

7 トップライン（履き口）の線はデザインに合わせて描きます。
Drawing the top line (where to put in foot) according to the design.

8 全体のバランスを整えて仕上げます。
Finishing by making nice balance for whole.

■Body Code

靴を描く／側面（ハイヒール） Drawing shoes/high heel (Profile/Side)

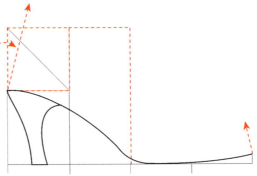

5 ヒール部分の上に正方形の当りをつけそのまま線を1/2線と交差させます。かかとはヒールの高い分、前屈状態になるため傾斜をつけておきます。
Drawing a reference square on the top of the heel part and intersect with a vertical line of the 1/2 on quartered line. Inclining a little because the heel part becomes anterior bending due to high heel.

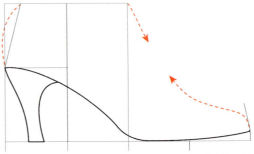

1 横に線を真っすぐ引き四等分して印をつけます。
Drawing a straight horizontal line and dividing it into four equal parts while putting marks.

6 かかとの丸みを描き1/2の交差した線からつま先の部分まで甲を包み込むように繋げて描きます。
Drawing the heel with roundness and drawing the line from 1/2 crossing line to the toe part as to wrap around the instep.

2 1/4にヒールの高さに合わせて目安線を描きます。
Drawing a reference line to 1/4 according to the heel height.

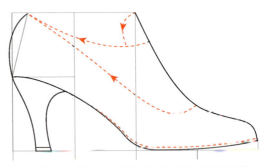

3 かかとから土踏まずにかけて足がアーチに気持ち良くのるようなイメージでラインを描きます。
Drawing a line from the heel to the arch of a foot with image of comfortable.

7 トップライン（履き口）の線はデザインに合わせて描きます。
Drawing the top line (where to put in foot) according to the design.

4 1/4部分を二等分した中心に合わせてヒールを描きます。
Drawing the heel on the center of the divided 1/4 part.

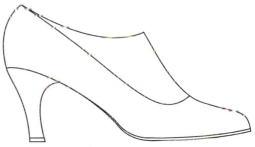

8 全体のバランスを整えて仕上げます。
Finishing by making nice balance for whole.

■Body Code

靴を描く／斜め（ローヒール・ハイヒール） Drawing shoes/high heel (Angled state)

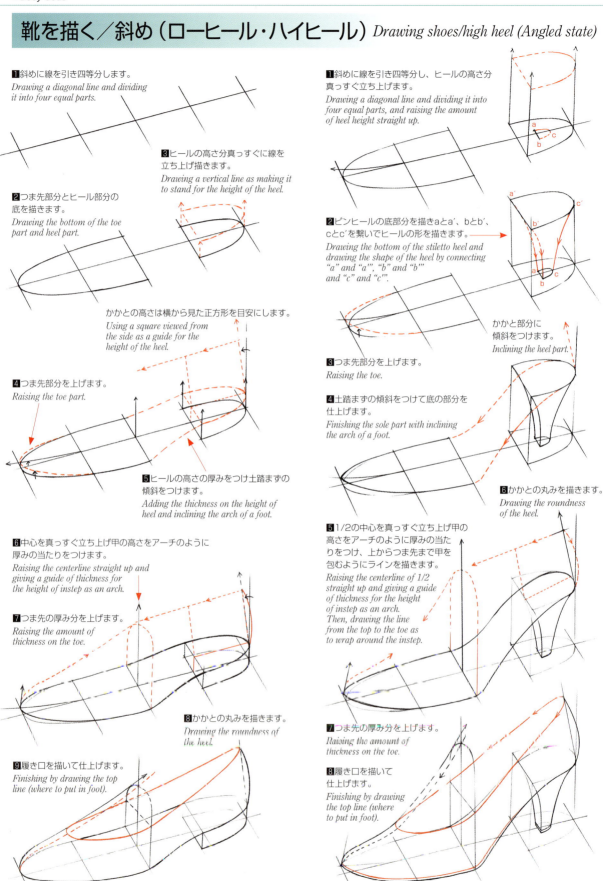

1 斜めに線を引き四等分します。
Drawing a diagonal line and dividing it into four equal parts.

2 つま先部分とヒール部分の底を描きます。
Drawing the bottom of the toe part and heel part.

3 ヒールの高さ分真っすぐに線を立ち上げ描きます。
Drawing a vertical line as making it to stand for the height of the heel.

かかとの高さは横から見た正方形を目安にします。
Using a square viewed from the side as a guide for the height of the heel.

4 つま先部分を上げます。
Raising the toe part.

5 ヒールの高さの厚みをつけ土踏まずの傾斜をつけます。
Adding the thickness on the height of heel and inclining the arch of a foot.

6 中心を真っすぐ立ち上げ甲の高さをアーチのように厚みの当たりをつけます。
Raising the centerline straight up and giving a guide of thickness for the height of instep as an arch.

7 つま先の厚み分を上げます。
Raising the amount of thickness on the toe.

8 かかとの丸みを描きます。
Drawing the roundness of the heel.

9 履き口を描いて仕上げます。
Finishing by drawing the top line (where to put in foot).

1 斜めに線を引き四等分し、ヒールの高さ分真っすぐ立ち上げます。
Drawing a diagonal line and dividing it into four equal parts, and raising the amount of heel height straight up.

2 ピンヒールの底部分を描きaとa'、bとb'、cとc'を繋いでヒールの形を描きます。
Drawing the bottom of the stiletto heel and drawing the shape of the heel by connecting "a" and "a'", "b" and "b'" and "c" and "c'".

かかと部分に傾斜をつけます。
Inclining the heel part.

3 つま先部分を上げます。
Raising the toe.

4 土踏まずの傾斜をつけて底の部分を仕上げます。
Finishing the sole part with inclining the arch of a foot.

5 1/2の中心を真っすぐ立ち上げ甲の高さをアーチのように厚みの当たりをつけ、上からつま先まで甲を包むようにラインを描きます。
Raising the centerline of 1/2 straight up and giving a guide of thickness for the height of instep as an arch. Then, drawing the line from the top to the toe as to wrap around the instep.

6 かかとの丸みを描きます。
Drawing the roundness of the heel.

7 つま先の厚み分を上げます。
Raising the amount of thickness on the toe.

8 履き口を描いて仕上げます。
Finishing by drawing the top line (where to put in foot).

■ 人体の法則

斜めに線を引き四等分する時に傾斜の付け方で見える角度が違ってきます
Showing different angles by the amount of the inclination when you draw a diagonal line and divide it into four equal parts.

■ スクエア・トウ
 Square toe

■ ポインテッド・トウ
 Pointed toe

■ ラウンド・トウ
 Round toe

底部分のシルエットで全体のイメージが変化します。
The whole image changes by the silhouette of the bottom part.

紐を描くとき、甲の中心から向こうと手前を回り込むように描くと立体的に見えます
When drawing shoelaces, showing more three-dimensional by drawing from the center of the instep to front side and back side as to wrap around.

ヒールの位置が少し前に入っているのが特徴のデザイン
The design has a characteristic that the position of the heel is put inside.

水彩の濃淡でエナメルの質感を描いています。白の色鉛筆とガッシュで光る部分を上から重ねて仕上げています
Painting the texture of enamel in watercolor shades. Finishing by painting the parts that shines on top by the white colored pencils and gouache.

87

■Body Code

靴を描く／いろいろな角度（ハイヒール） *Drawing shoes/high heel (Various angles)*

正面や後ろからの角度も基本の4分割を目安にするとバランスよく描くことができます。
Any angles from the front or back can also be drawn in a well-balanced manner by using a baseline that is divided into four equal parts as a guide.

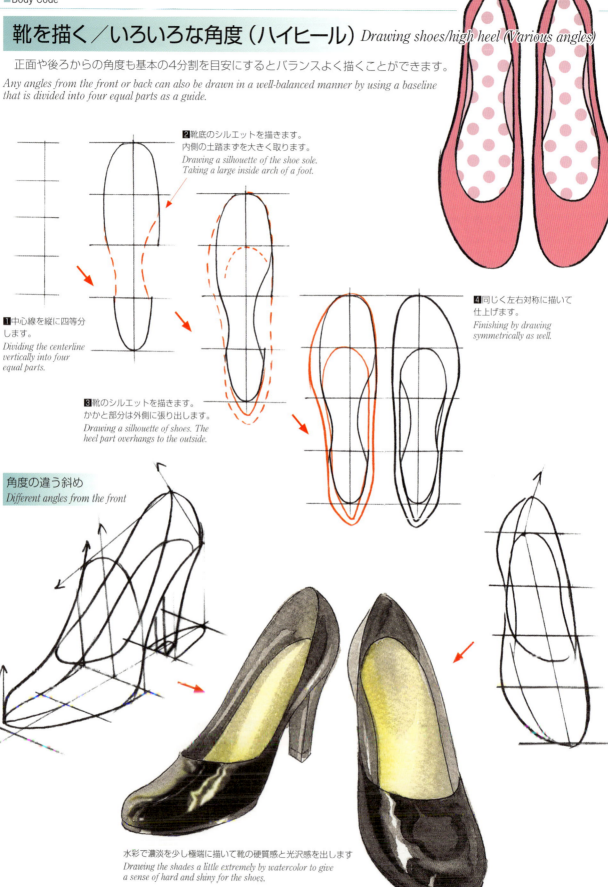

②靴底のシルエットを描きます。内側の土踏まずを大きく取ります。
Drawing a silhouette of the shoe sole. Taking a large inside arch of a foot.

①中心線を縦に四等分します。
Dividing the centerline vertically into four equal parts.

③靴のシルエットを描きます。かかと部分は外側に張り出します。
Drawing a silhouette of shoes. The heel part overhangs to the outside.

④同じく左右対称に描いて仕上げます。
Finishing by drawing symmetrically as well.

角度の違う斜め
Different angles from the front

水彩で濃淡を少し極端に描いて靴の硬質感と光沢感を出します
Drawing the shades a little extremely by watercolor to give a sense of hard and shiny for the shoes.

88

■ 人体の法則

斜め後ろ
Different angles from the back

ヒールが高くなると体重が前に移動するため、
かかとの傾斜も深くなります
Inclining the heel strongly when it becomes higher and the weight moves to the front.

1 斜めにまっすぐ線を引き四等分します。
Drawing a straight line diagonally and dividing it into four equal parts.

2 靴底のシルエットを描きヒールの
高さまでまっすぐ線を立ち上げます。
Drawing a silhouette of the shoe sole and drawing a straight line vertically as it stands as same as the height of the heel.

3 かかとから土踏まずにかけてラインを描き、
ヒールが高い場合はつま先部分まで傾斜をつけます。
Drawing a line from heel to arch of a foot, and inclining the line to the toe part if the heel is high.

4 厚底の場合は先に底の厚さ分を立ち上げ、
その部分からつま先の厚み分を描きます。
In the case of thick sole, raising the line for the thickness of the sole first, and drawing the thickness of the toe from the part.

水彩で薄く下地の色をつけ、よく乾いた後にパステルで濃淡をつけます。
白のパステルと色鉛筆で強く光を反射している部分を描いて仕上げます
Applying a base color lightly by watercolors and adding shades by pastel after it dried well. Finishing by painting the parts that reflect brightly by the white colored pencils and pastel.

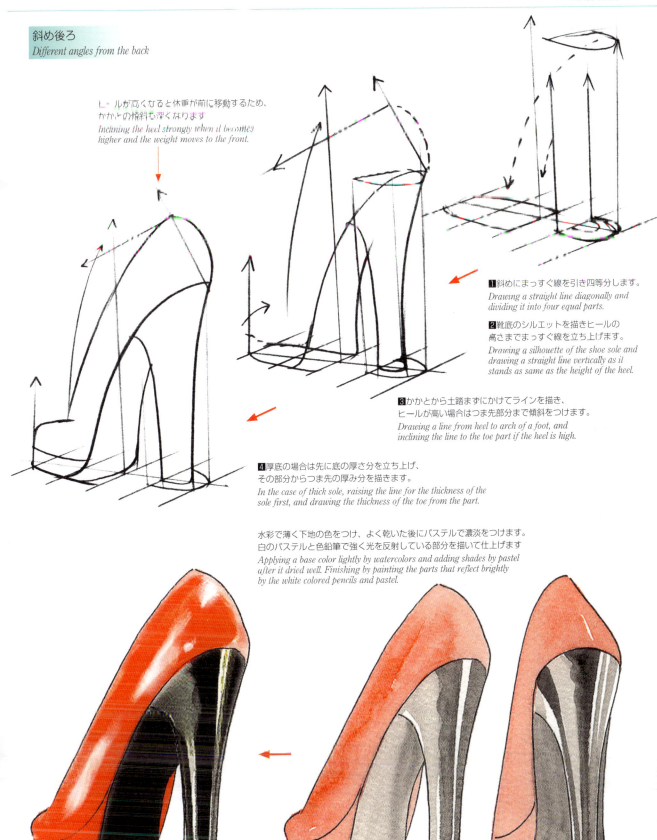

89

■Body Code

ドレープを描く *Drawing a drape*

　ドレープは、布をたらしたときに出るゆるやかなひだやたるみのことです。コスチュームを描くとき素材感やデザインの特徴を示す重要な要素になります。体にまとわせた時にどのように見えるか、生地の風合いや性質で大きく変わります。柔らかい布は流れるようにドレープを生み出し、硬い布は張りが出たシルエットになります。

Drape is a gentle slacks or folds that occurs when you hang a cloth. It is one of the important elements that shows the texture and design features when you draw costumes. The looks of it changes drastically depending on the texture and nature of the fabric when the body wears it. Soft fabric makes drapes as it likes flowing, and hard fabric shows a silhouette firmly.

四角い布地の真ん中を始点に一ヶ所でたらします
Hanging the square fabric by a point on the middle of it.

四角い布地の端を始点にバイヤスでたらします
Hanging the square fabric by a point on the corner of it with bias angle.

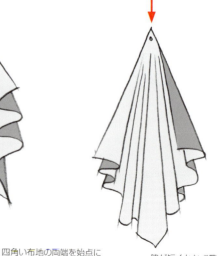

脇が長くなります
The sides get longer.

脇が短くなります
The sides get shorter.

四角い布地の両端を始点に一ヶ所でたらします
Hanging the square fabric by the two points of edge.

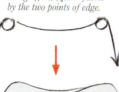

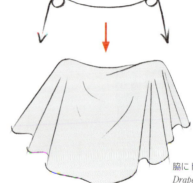

脇にドレープがたまります
Drapes gather on the sides.

90

■ 人体の法則

重なったドレープ　*Overlapped drapes*

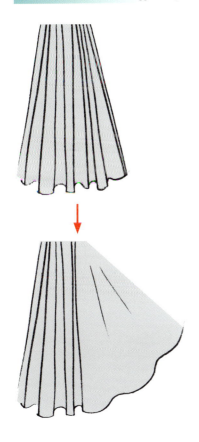

サーキュラー型のドレープ　*Circular drapes*

横位置　*Horizontal position*　　　縦位置　*Vertical position*

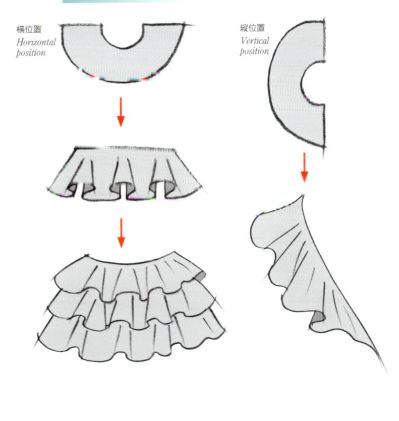

ギャザーを寄せたドレープ　*Gathered drape*

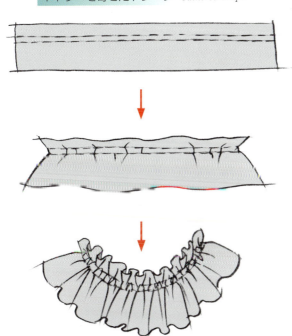

古代ギリシャの衣裳は、布をそのまま体に巻き付けたもので、いかに美しいドレープを作るかが着こなしの基本でした。その後もひだは重要視され上流階級の貴族になるほど、ひだをたくさん用い、ひだを贅沢に使うことは権威の象徴にもなったのです。

The basics of dressing for ancient Greek costumes were how much beautiful drapes that people are able to make with fabric wrapped around the body. People had given importance to the folds even after that. Aristocrats of the upper class used more and more numbers of the folds and the luxury uses of folds became a symbol of authority.

91

■Body Code

ドレープと柄の動き *Movement of drapes and patterns*

　ドレープの動きによって柄は大きく変化します。例えばストライプ（縦縞）は途中からボーダー（横縞）になり水玉も歪んで変化します。

The patterns change greatly depending on the movement of the drape. For example, vertical stripes become horizontal stripes along the way and polka dots are distorted and changed.

ストライプ　*Stripes*

ストライプ＆ボーダー　*Vertical stripes & Horizontal stripes*

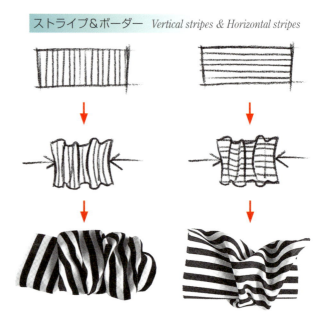

ボーダー　*Horizontal stripes*

■ 人体の法則

水玉　*Polka dot*

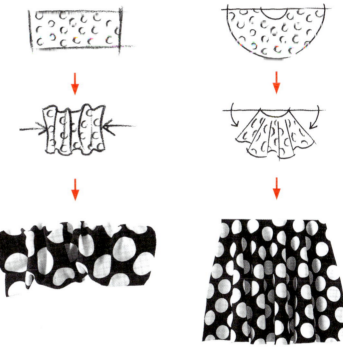

正円が立体的な筒状になった場合、
両サイドに向かって楕円になっていきます
The precise circle becomes ellipse towards both sides when it is drawn as a three-dimensional cylindrical shape.

一見、複雑に見える柄も単純な形に置き換えて、位置や大きさの
バランスを見ながら当たりをとり細部を描いていきます
Replacing the pattern that looks seemingly complicated with a simple shape, and giving a rough guide while checking the balance between size and placement, then drawing the details.

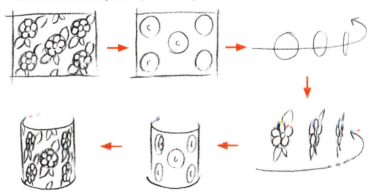

93

■Body Code

ポーズバリエーション *Pose variation*

　エスキース（下絵）の段階でポーズを考えるとき、いちばん大切にしたいことは、服の持つエスプリ（精神）が伝わることやデザインが魅力的に見えることです。ボリュームのある服を軽快に見せたいときは動きのあるポーズが効果的ですし、細身のスカートやエレガントなスタイルには静的な中にも片足重心でバランスをとったポーズが魅力的です。

The thing that is the most important when you think about the pose on the phase of Esquisse (rough sketches) is expressing the Esprit (spirit) of the garment and showing attractive point of design. Poses with movement are effective when you want to show a garment with volume lightly, and the poses with weight bearing on one leg that has calm image, are attractive when you draw slender skirts and elegant styles.

片足重心で腰のラインを強調したエレガントなポーズ
An elegant pose that emphasizes the line of the waist with weight bearing on one leg.

内股ポーズでキュートに！
Making it cute with pigeon-toed pose!

パンツラインを表現しやすい、遠近をつけた片足重心ポーズ
A pose with weight bearing on one leg that has perspective, for easy to express the pants line.

■ 人体の法則

ウォーキングポーズで
自然な躍動感！
*Natural uplifting
feeling with walking
pose!*

足を内股気味にしたポーズ
で可愛らしさが
*Adding cute image with a
little bit pigeon-toed pose*

95

■Body Code

シンプルな服も
リズム感のある
ポーズで
Expressing by a rhythmic pose even it is simple clothes

下から見上げて大胆な
遠近感のあるポーズ
A bold pose with perspective that is looked up from below

■ 人体の法則

真っすぐの立ちポーズは
胸をぐっと張らせて
*A straight standing pose
with pumping up the chest.*

第3章
着色しよう

デザインのイメージを決定づけるとき
素材や配色は非常に大きな要素です。
エスキース（下絵）の段階では思いどおりの
イメージで描けていたのに
彩色すると無惨な結果になることがよくあります。
それは道具が介在すればする程
技術が必要となるからですが
用紙の種類や画材の性質を知ることで
かなり解消されます。
彩色することで生き生きと広がる
ドローイングの世界を楽しみましょう。

Chapter 3
Give Coloring (Try coloring)

The materials and the color schemes are very important factors when the image of design is determined. Although it was well drawn in the ideal image at the phase of Esquisse (rough sketches), it is often happened that disastrous results are created after the coloring step. It is because the more techniques are required if there are many variation of materials. However, you are able to solve the most of those by knowing types of paper and characteristics of the painting tools. Let's enjoy the world of drawing that vividly and lively spreads by coloring.

Water color

水彩で描く
Drawing with Watercolor

水彩用具

筆使いであらゆる表現ができる水彩絵の具は、欠かすことのできない画材の一つです。水彩絵の具には、透明水彩とガッシュ（不透明水彩）の二つのタイプがあります。

透明水彩の特色は重ねて塗った下の色が透けて見え、下の色と上に重ねた色との効果で微妙に変化し、透明感のある仕上がりになることです。ガッシュは不透明で、重ね塗りすると下の色がかくれるので、グラデーション使いや濃淡の扱い時、タッチや厚塗り、水で溶いた普通の水彩絵の具としても使えるなど、多様性と修正がしやすい利点があります。

Watercolor painting tools

Watercolor paint that is able to make every various expression by brushwork, is one of the indispensable painting tools. There are two types of watercolor paints that are transparent watercolor and gouache (opaque watercolor). The characteristics of transparent watercolor are that the lower color can be seen through the upper color, and it changes slightly by the effect of the lower color and the color that is superimposed. It can make a finish with transparent feeling as the result. As the gouache is opaque, and the lower color disappears when it is superimposed. It can be used as a gradation expression, impasto, an even touch expression without contrasted density, and as a regular watercolor paint if it is diluted with water as well. It means that there are advantages that is easy to correct and functional versatility.

❶水彩（チューブ）Watercolor (Tube type) ❷ケーキカラー（乾）固形水彩絵の具 Cake Color (Dry) Solid watercolor ❸顔彩絵の具 Gansai pigment ❹カラーインク Color ink ❺アクリル絵の具 Acrylic paint ❻筆洗 Brush washer ❼絵皿 Palette ❽筆 Painting brush ❾刷毛 Brush

水彩用紙　Various Papers for Watercolor

❶アルシュ紙（荒目）、❷アルシュ紙（細目）：フランス製の高級水彩紙で、素材は100％コットンの中性紙。手漉きに近い製法で製造されておりナチュラルホワイトで、消しゴムで消しても毛羽立たない強い紙肌を持ち水彩、パステル、色鉛筆などに最適です。

ARCHES (ROUGH), ARCHES (FINE): A French high-quality watercolor paper made of 100% cotton neutralized paper. It is manufactured by a method close to hand-made, and is natural white colored. It has a strong paper skin that does not make hairy surface even if rubbed with an eraser. It is an ideal paper for watercolors, pastels and colored pencils, etc.

❸ファブリアーノ紙：イタリア製の高級水彩紙で、100％コットンの中性紙、美しい白さがあり発色に優れ、描きやすい適度な水の吸い込み、ひっかきにも耐える丈夫さが特徴で水彩、パステル、色鉛筆などに最適です。

FABRIANO: An Italian high-quality watercolor paper, made of 100% cotton neutralized paper with beautiful white color that produces great colors. It is eminently suitable for watercolor, pastel and colored pencils as it has characteristics such as moderate water absorption for drawing easily and toughness enough to withstand scratching.

❹ワトソン水彩紙：英国製の高級水彩紙で、100％コットンの中性紙、柔らかな風合いと、発色の生きる白さが特長で水彩、パステル、色鉛筆などに最適です。

WATSON Watercolor: A British high-quality watercolor paper made of 100% cotton neutralized paper. It is eminently suitable for watercolor, pastel and colored pencils as it has characteristics of soft texture and white color that produces great colors.

❺キャンソン紙：中性で水に強く描画後も波打ちが少ない水彩紙。ナチュラルホワイトで発色が非常によく独特なラフ肌で、水彩、チャコール、パステル、マーカーに優れています。

CANSON: A watercolor paper that is neutral and strong in water does not cause wavy effect much after drawing.It is natural-white colored paper that produces great colors, and has distinctive rough surfaces that is eminently suitable for watercolor, charcoal pencil, pastel and marker.

❻BBケント紙：表面が滑らかで目が細かく、ボタニカルアートのような細密画やペン画マーカー、鉛筆等の表現に適している。また適度な吸水性があり、細かい作業で何度も筆を重ねても表面が弱りません。

BB KENT: The surface is smooth and fine-grained, and it is suitable for delicate expressions of marker pens, pencils and miniature painting like a botanical art. In addition, it has moderate water absorption, and also has toughness that the surface does not get damaged even if fine work with brushes is repeated many times.

❼ケント紙：表面に弾力性を持たせてあるため、鉛筆やインク、マーカーなどののりが良く、にじみもなく、発色も良い。また、消しゴムによる毛羽立ちがないので、製図・カンプ・版下・建築パースなどに最適です。

KENT: It works well with pencils, inks, and markers, and produces good colors without bleeding, because the surface has elasticity. In addition, it is the most suitable for drafting, comprehensive layout, block copy, and architecture perspective drawings because there is no hairy texture caused by eraser.

❽マーメイド紙：荒目の紙肌を持つ紙で、独特なラフ肌は、水彩、チャコール、パステルに優れ、また強靭な紙肌で、毛羽立ちがありません。

MERMAID: This paper has surface with rough texture and the unique rough surface works well with watercolor, charcoal pencil, and pastel. In addition, it is also strong surface against rubbing without fuzz texture

丸筆（太）Round paint brush (Thick)
丸筆（中）Round paint brush (Medium)
丸筆（細）Round paint brush (Thin)
面相筆 Fine-point brush
平筆 Flat paint brush
アクリル平筆 Flat acrylic paint brush
ぼかし筆 Blurring brush

■Give Coloring

ショートヘアを描く／目を描く *Drawing Short hair / Drawing Eyes*

1肌色の一番明るい色で顔全体を薄く均一に塗ります。目と眉の間、鼻の下、下唇の下、首の下、顔の輪郭部分は影になるので濃く塗ります。

Applying the brightest color of the skin tone onto the entire face lightly and evenly. Applying darker color between the eyes and eyebrows, under the nose, under the lower lip, under the neck, the outline of the face because there are shaded.

2髪は顔に比べて色が強いため、濃くなりがちなので注意します。肌色が乾いたあとに髪の一番明るい色から塗ります。ウエーブの盛り上がっている部分は光るので白く残しながら軽く濃淡をつけます。

Must be careful about the hair color because it has stronger color than the face and tends to be darker. Applying the color from the brightest one of the hair after the skin color is dry. Applying the shading lightly while leaving white on the raised part of the wave hair because it glows under the light.

3両サイドの付け根や髪の流れによる影の部分に濃淡をつけて立体感を出します。

Adding shading to the part with shadows that is caused by flowing hair and the base of hairs on the both side, to create a three-dimensional effect.

1輪郭を描きます。
Drawing an outline

 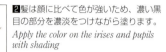

2髪は顔に比べて色が強いため、濃い黒目の部分を濃淡をつけながら塗ります。
Apply the color on the irises and pupils with shading

3瞳を黒く塗ります。
Applying the black color more to pupil

4瞳と黒目の部分に瞳に向かって放射線状に白く光を入れて仕上げます。
Finishing with applying white radial lines on the irises and white dot on the pupil, as an expression of lights.

4水彩でのメークは、自然な仕上がり感がポイント。頬紅はチークの場所により、ひとまわり大きく水を引いてぼかしながらなじむように塗ります。このとき、水を引いた際まで広がると乾いたときシミになるので注意します。影となる上唇は濃く塗り、下唇は艶を出すため白く残して光沢感を出します。

The point of make-up expression in watercolor is a finishing with natural feeling. Applying colors of the blusher that is related on a location of cheek, with fitting and blurring after putting water on a part larger than the size of cheek. At this time, must be careful that it does not spread to the edge of water part because it becomes a stain when it gets dry. Applying darker color on the upper lip that is in shadow parts, and leaving white part on the lower lip to give it a glossy feeling.

使用画材［ガッシュ・固形水彩ケーキカラー（乾）・アルシュ紙（細目）］
Materials Used [Gouache · Cake Color (Dry) Solid watercolor · ARCHES (FINE)]

■着色しよう

ミディアムヘアを描く／口を描く Drawing Medium hair / Drawing a Mouth

1 濃淡をつけながら肌を塗ります。
Applying the color on the skin with shading.

2 肌色が充分に乾いた後、濃淡をつけながら髪を塗ります。
Applying the color on the hair with shading after the skin color is dry enough.

3 全体の調子を見ながらウエーブにそって濃淡をつけます。このとき、髪が重くなり過ぎないように根元は濃く毛先は軽く描きます。
Applying the shading along the movement of hair waves, while checking the overall tone. At this time, the base of hair is dark and the tips of hair are lightly drawn to not make the hair heavy too much.

4 深い影が出る顔の側面から首元に向かって濃く描き加えます。
Adding darker color from the side of the face where the deep shadows appear towards to the neck.

5 水彩で仕上げるメークはむらになりやすいため、パウダー状のパステル、チーク、アイシャドーなどメーク用具で仕上げると簡単で効果的。細かい部分は擦筆（サッピツ）でこすってていねいに仕上げます。
It is easy and effective to finish by coloring the shadows on the parts of make-up with pastels or make-up tools because the part by watercolor gets uneven color easily. Applying the color on the fine parts of the make-up delicately with a Tortillon that is made from a hard paper.

1 輪郭を描きます。
Drawing an outline

2 唇の輪郭に沿って濃く塗ります。
Applying the color strongly along the outline of the lip.

3 口紅の光沢感を残しながらぼかし立体感を出します。
Giving a three-dimensional effect by blurring, while leaving the glossy feeling of the lipstick.

使用画材［ガッシュ・固形水彩ケーキカラー（乾）・アルシュ紙（細目）］
Materials Used [Gouache · Cake Color (Dry) Solid watercolor · ARCHES (FINE)]

■Give Coloring

ロングヘアを描く *Drawing Long hair*

■ストレート *Straight*

❶ストレートヘアを描く時は毛先が重くならないように注意します。
Must be careful not to make the tips of hair heavy when you draw the straight hair.

❷最初に肌色を明るく均一に塗ります。
Applying the color of the skin brightly and evenly first.

❸光沢部分を白く残しながら薄く塗り、髪の流れに沿って濃淡をつけます。
Applying the color along the flowing of hair with shading, while coloring the glossy part lightly with leaving white part.

❹充分に乾いた後、明るい色で光沢部分を塗り重ねます。
Applying the bright color on top for the glossy part after sufficient drying.

❺最後にメークを施し仕上げます。
Finishing by putting on make-up at the end.

106

■着色しよう

■ウエーブ Wavy

1 ウエーブのかかったロングヘアは、髪の流れがどの部分から流れているかに注意しながら肌色を明るく均一に塗ります。
Applying the color of the skin brightly and evenly with being careful to understand which parts the hair flows from, when you draw wavy long hair.

2 ウエーブのボリュームがある部分を白く残しながら薄く塗ります。
Applying the color lightly while leaving the volume part of the wave white.

3 ウエーブに沿って影の部分を濃く塗ります。
Applying darker color on the shadow parts along the waves of hair.

4 最後にメークを描き入れます。ここではメイク用具のチークで仕上げています。
Finishing by putting on make-up with using the blusher of the make-up tool at the end.

使用画材［ガッシュ・固形水彩ケーキカラー（乾）・アルシュ紙（中目）］
Materials Used [Gouache・Cake Color (Dry) Solid watercolor・ARCHES (MEDIUM)]

■ Give Coloring

単色で立体感を出す Creating a three-dimensional effect for a single color

不透明水彩でしっかり彩色する基本の地塗りです。光の方向を意識して影の部分は濃く、光の方向は薄く塗り、濃・中・淡で立体感を出します。

This is a basic skill of ground painting that is for coloring firmly with opaque watercolors. While considering the direction of the light, applying darker color on the part of the shadow, lighter color on the direction of the light. Making a three-dimensional effect by using shades in dark, medium and light.

①最初に薄く肌色を塗ります。
Applying the color of the skin lightly first.

②薄地の素材感はガッシュに水をたっぷり含ませて、薄く塗ることで軽さを出します。
Creating lightness by lightly applying gouache that is added plenty of water, for the texture of light fabric.

③髪はブラウスの色を塗ったあとに塗ります。
Applying the color on hair after coloring to the blouse.

④ドレープの重なりを確認しながら、影の部分を濃く塗ります。
Applying darker color to the part of the shadow while checking the overlap of drapes.

重心がかかっている方の腰位置が高くなり布地が引っ張られます
The fabric is pulled because the waist position on weight-bearing side rises.

⑤身頃のドレープ部分は自然光を意識し片側を濃く濃・中・淡で強弱を出して塗ります。
Applying the color on the drape part of the body with adjusting the shades in dark, medium and light, while concerning natural light and applying darker color on the one side.

⑥裾のレース部分はブラウスと同じように薄く塗り充分に乾いた後レースの柄を面相筆で入れます。
Applying the color on the lace part of the hem lightly as same as a blouse coloring, and putting the pattern of the lace by a fine-point brush after sufficient drying.

108

■着色しよう

ヘアは重くならないように軽めに塗るのがコツです
The point is applying the color on the hair lightly to not make it heavy.

透明水彩のように薄く塗り乾いた後にもう一度、少し濃い色で髪の流れに沿い塗り重ねます
Applying a little darker color again along the flowing of hair, after applying the color lightly likes a transparent watercolor, and sufficient drying.

布地の重なっている部分は濃く塗ります
Applying darker color on the part of the fabric overlapping.

ハイライトを入れることでツヤ感と立体感が出ます
Giving a sense of sheen and the three-dimensional effect by putting the highlight.

影の部分を少し暗めの色で重ね塗りします
Overpainting with a slightly darker color onto the part of shadow.

裾のレース部分はブラウスと同じ様に薄く塗り充分に乾いた後、レースの柄を面相筆で入れます
Applying the color on the lace part of the hem lightly as same as a blouse coloring, and putting the pattern of the lace by a fine-point brush after sufficient drying.

中心部分を明るく表現することで丸みのある立体感が表現できます
It can express a rounded three-dimensional effect by expressing the central part brightly.

最後に白の色鉛筆でドレープのハイライトを入れて仕上げる。
Finishing with putting highlight of drape by white colored pencil at the end.

Q & A

濃くなり過ぎて立体感や形が出なくなった場合は？
What if the color gets dark too much and does not show a three-dimensional effect or shape?

❶たっぷり水を含ませた筆で色を浮き上がらせる。
Making the color float up with a brush that contains plenty of water.

❷浮き上がった色をペーパータオルで拭き取り充分に乾かす。
Wiping up the color came up, with a paper towel and dry sufficiently.

❸再度、色を塗り白の色鉛筆で仕上げる。
Applying the color again and finishing by adding white colored pencil.

使用画材［ガッシュ・色鉛筆・アルシュ紙（細目）］
Materials Used [Gouache · Colored pencil · ARCHES (FINE)]

■Give Coloring

透ける素材を描く *Drawing Transparent materials/fabrics*

墨入れをします。このときに、エスキースをそのまま写すのではなく新たに線を引く気持ちで描きます
Putting inks. At this time, drawing a line with a feeling of drawing a new line instead of just tracing the line of Esquisse (rough sketches).

❶丸筆で肌色をしっかり塗ります。透明感のあるブラウスと重なる部分も同じ調子で塗ります。
Applying the color of skin firmly with a round paint brush. Applying the same tone onto the part that is overlapping the blouse that has a sense of transparency.

❷インナーは濃く塗りブラウスと重なる部分は一段落として薄く塗ります。布地のキワは光るのでハイライトとして白く残しておきます。
Applying darker color on the part of inner garment, and applying a little lighter color onto the part that is overlapping the blouse. Leaving the edge of the fabric white as a highlight because it glows.

エスキース（下絵）の段階でラフにデザインポイントやバランスなどの構想を考えます
Thinking about the design concepts such as design points and balances roughly, on the phase of Esquisse (rough sketches).

❸充分に乾いた後にブラウスの色を全体に薄く塗り、重なる部分や影の部分は薄いブルーグレーで塗り重ねます。
Applying the color of blouse to the whole part of it lightly after sufficient drying. Overpainting on the part overlapping and the part of shadows with the color of pale blue gray.

■着色しよう

④丸筆で強弱をつけながら絵柄を描きます。
Drawing a pattern with a round paint brush, while adjusting strength and weakness of touches.

⑤柄の奥行きは色の濃淡で表現します。
Expressing the perspective of pattern by shading of color.

⑥最後に面相筆を使って影の部分を少し濃く塗り、白のガッシュでハイライトを入れて仕上げます。
Finishing by applying the color a little darker on the part of shadow with using a fine-point brush, and putting highlights by white gouache at the end.

使用画材［ガッシュ・色鉛筆・アルシュ紙（細目）］
Materials Used [Gouache · Colored pencil · ARCHES (FINE)]

● Give Coloring

モアレ模様を描く *Drawing the Moiré Pattern*

❶ 斜め上からの自然光を意識して肌色を塗ります。
Applying the color of skin while concerning natural light from obliquely upward.

※足の動きに沿ってドレープを描き量感を出します
Drawing a drape along the movement of the legs to give a sense of volume.

❸ 丸筆で強弱をつけながらモアレ模様を薄く描きます。
Drawing Moiré pattern lightly with a round paint brush while adjusting strength and weakness of touches.

❷ 白地に柄を入れるときは、後から影を入れると色が溶けて画面が汚れてしまいます。初めにブルーグレーで軽く影を入れておきます。
When you draw patterns on a white background, it gets dirty on the screen by melting colors if you add a shadow later. Applying the color of blue gray onto shadow part lightly at the beginning.

■Give Coloring

エナメルを描く　*Drawing the Enamel*

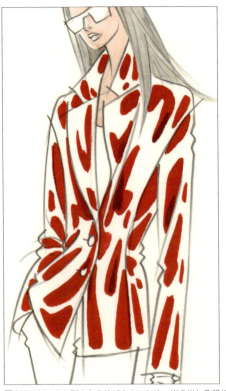

❶光沢素材は光と影の色の差が大きいため、光の当たる部分を白く抜きながらエナメル独特のぬめり感が出るように不規則に塗ります。複雑で汚い仕上がりになりがちですが、構造線のキワに沿って塗るとくっきりとした立体感のあるラインが出ます。
Applying the color irregularly to show a unique slimy feel of enamel while leaving the parts that is lighted white, as glossy materials have a large difference in color between light and shadow. Although it tends to be a complicated and dirty finish, it shows a clear three-dimensional line if you apply the color along the edge of structure lines.

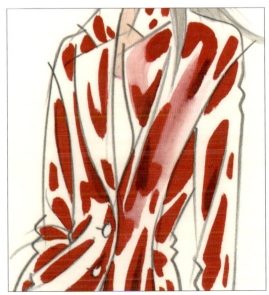

❷水を含ませた筆で溶かすように塗ります。
Applying the color with dissolving by a brush containing water.

■着色しよう

❸均一に塗るのではなくランダムなタッチを生かして、なじませたり残したりしながら塗ります。
Applying the color with blending or leaving the color by using random touches instead of evenly applying.

❹最後に白のガッシュでハイライトを入れて仕上げます。
Finishing by adding highlights with white gouache at the end.

❺パンツは斜めからの自然光を意識して、光の当たる部分は薄く、影の部分を濃く、濃・中・淡で立体的に仕上げます。
Applying lighter color on the part that is lighted, darker color on the part of the shadow while concerning natural light from obliquely upward, for the pants. Finishing by creating a three dimensional effect with shading in dark, medium and light.

使用画材［ガッシュ・色鉛筆・アルシュ紙（細目）］
Materials Used [Gouache・Colored pencil・ARCHES (FINE)]

115

■Give Coloring

ヘリンボーンを描く *Drawing the pattern of Herringbone*

■布地の方向性に注意しなが
ら地の目に沿って縦線を軽く
引きます。
*Drawing vertical lines lightly
along the grain line of fabric
while paying attention to the
direction of the fabric.*

②杉綾の幅に縦線を描きます。
*Drawing vertical lines on the
width of the Herringbone.*

■着色しよう

3 平筆を斜めに持ちランダムに斜線（杉綾）を入れます。このときに縦線からはみ出すくらいの気持ちで描くと織の表情が出ます。
Drawing diagonal lines (Herringbone) randomly with holding a flat brush diagonally. At this time, it shows better expression of the weaving if you draw with a feeling that the diagonal lines can go out a little from the vertical lines.

4 平筆を斜め逆に持ち替えて、縦線の間をハの字のように描きます。
Drawing diagonal lines that are shaped inverted V-shape in between vertical lines with holding the flat brush diagonally in opposite way.

5 描いた後でもう少し影の部分を濃くしたい場合は薄いグレーマーカーで塗り足します。
Adding a light gray marker lightly if you want to make the part of shadow a bit darker after the drawing.

使用画材［ガッシュ・色鉛筆・アルシュ紙（細目）］
Materials Used [Gouache · Colored pencil · ARCHES (FINE)]

ラメ素材を描く *Drawing the Lamé (Glitter) materials/fabrics*

1 明るい色を中心にドレス全体を濃淡で地塗りします。ベルベットのような重厚な光沢感を意識して仕上げるのがコツです。

Applying the base color to the entire dress with shading, centering on bright colors. The point is to finish by concerning with a sense of heavy and glossy like Velvet.

■着色しよう

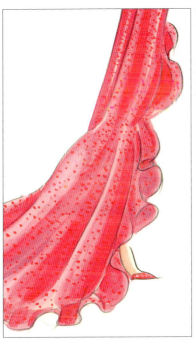

2 面相筆で全体に地塗りの色と同色でラメの部分を描き入れます（軽く不規則に）。
Drawing the Lamé (Glitter) in the same color as the base color onto the entire dress with a fine-point brush. (Lightly and irregularly).

3 地の色より一段濃い色でラメを描き加えて深みを出します。
Drawing the additional Lamé (Glitter) in a darker color than the base color to make more richness.

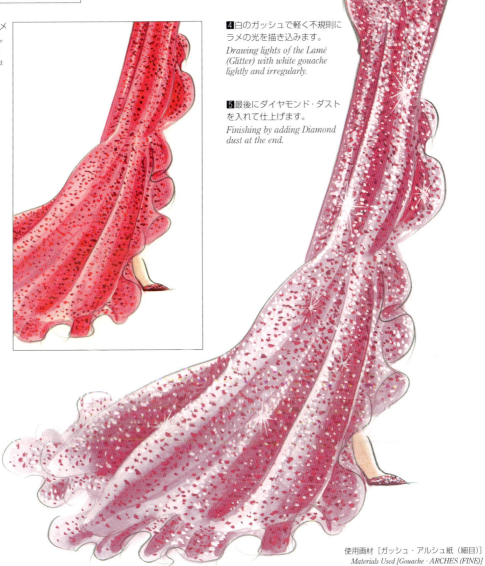

4 白のガッシュで軽く不規則にラメの光を描き込みます。
Drawing lights of the Lamé (Glitter) with white gouache lightly and irregularly.

5 最後にダイヤモンド・ダストを入れて仕上げます。
Finishing by adding Diamond dust at the end.

使用画材［ガッシュ・アルシュ紙（細目）］
Materials Used [Gouache・ARCHES (FINE)]

■ Give Coloring

千鳥格子を描く *Drawing the pattern of Houndstooth*

千鳥格子Ⅰ　*Houndstooth I*　　　　　　　　　　千鳥格子Ⅱ　*Houndstooth II*

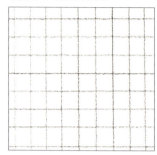 

❶格子の大きさに合わせて鉛筆で軽く目安となる縦線と横線を引きます。
Drawing vertical and horizontal lines lightly as a guide by a pencil, according to the size of the Houndstooth.

❶地塗りが充分に乾いた後、鉛筆で軽く目安となる縦線と横線を引きます。平筆を斜めに持ち、ひと目おきにダイヤ柄を入れます。
Drawing vertical and horizontal lines lightly as a guide by a pencil after the base paint has dried sufficiently. Drawing diamond patterns on every second grid with holding the flat brush diagonally.

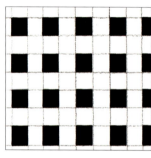 

❷ひと目おきに格子を塗ります。（ナイロン平筆を使うとエッジが効くので簡単）
Applying the color on every second grid. (It is easy to paint with using nylon flat brush since the edge works well.)

❷平筆を斜めに持ったまま右上に斜線を入れます。
Drawing diagonal lines on the top right with holding the flat brush diagonally.

❸平筆を斜めに持ち牙の部分を描きます。
Drawing the parts of fangs (teeth) with holding the flat brush diagonally.

❸次に左下に斜線を入れます。
Drawing diagonal lines on the lower left, next.

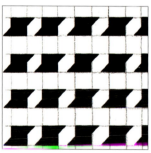 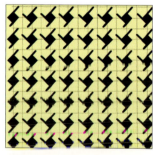

❹同じように右上の牙の部分を描きます。
Drawing the parts of fangs (teeth) on the top right in the same way.

❹平筆を持ち替えて同じように左上に斜線を入れます。
In the same way, Drawing diagonal lines on the top left with holding the brush reversely.

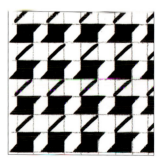

❺格子の間に斜線を入れて仕上げます。
Finishing by adding diagonal lines between the painted grids.

❺右下に斜線を入れて仕上げます。
Finishing by drawing diagonal lines on the lower right at the end.

■着色しよう

1 千鳥格子の大きさに合わせて鉛筆で軽く目安となる縦線と横線を引きます。
Drawing vertical and horizontal lines lightly as a guide by a pencil, according to the size of the Houndstooth.

2 エッジの利くナイロン平筆で、ひと目おきに格子を塗ります。
Applying the color on every second grid by using a nylon flat brush with good edge work.

3 ナイロン平筆を斜めに持ちランダムに斜線を入れます。
Drawing the diagonal lines randomly with holding a nylon flat brush diagonally.

使用画材［ガッシュ・色鉛筆・アルシュ紙（細目）］
Materials Used [Gouache · Colored pencil · ARCHES (FINE)]

Give Coloring

ファーを描く *Drawing the Fur*

1 ファーはたっぷりとボリューム感のある
シルエットで描き、アウトラインは毛足が
感じられるように軽く描きます。
*Drawing outline lightly for expressing
a feeling of hair on the fur
while drawing it with
voluminous silhouette.*

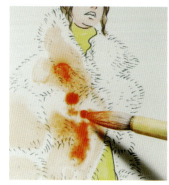

3 たっぷりの水を引き丸筆で先に明るい色
をたらし込み、次に濃い色でぼかしながら
濃淡をつけます。
*Applying a bright color first with a round
brush that contains plenty of water, then
adding the shads while blurring with a
darker color next.*

2 インナーのセーターとパンツの色
を先に着色します。ファーの毛足が
重なる部分は少し薄く塗ります。
*Applying the color of the inner
sweater and pants first. Applying
the color lightly to the parts that
hair of fur is overlapping.*

応用表現
ムートンやボア素材もアウトラインを変えて地塗りはぼかします。充分
に乾いたあとに同色のパステルで塗り足すと深みのあるムートンになり
ます。ボアの場合はファーと同じように毛足を描き足します。
*Advanced expression
Changing the outline and blurring the base paint for expressing both
Mouton and Boa fabric/material. After sufficiently drying it, painting
with the same color pastel to make a rich Mouton. For the Boa,
adding hair of the Boa by drawing in the same way as the fur.*

4 ファーの地塗りはフラットにならないよ
うにします。ぼかすことで毛足の微妙な動
きによる光り方を感じさせます。
*Making sure the base paint of the fur should
not become flat. Expressing the reflecting
feeling of the subtle movement on the fur,
by blurring.*

122

■着色しよう

ぼかしの地塗りと毛足の描き込みの相乗効果で微妙な動きと光を感じさせます。
Expressing the subtle movement and light, by the synergetic effect of the detail drawing of hair and blurred base paint.

⑤極細の面相筆を使い、明るい色の部分は同色の濃淡で毛足を描きます。
Drawing hair of the fur on the bright parts with shading of the same color by using the extra-fine-point brush.

⑥濃い色の部分も同色の濃淡で毛足を描き根気よく丁寧に描くことでファーのゴージャス感が表現できます
Expressing the gorgeous feeling of the fur by drawing hair for the darker part with shading of the same color, carefully and perseveringly.

⑦最後に白で毛足の光沢を描き入れて仕上げます。白はジンクホワイトでは強すぎて毛足が硬くなりやすいためパールホワイトを混ぜて柔らかさを出します。
Finishing by drawing the gloss of hair with white at the end. Making soft texture by mixing Pearl White, as Zinc White is too strong and it makes the fur harder.

重なる部分を表現することで分量感が出ます。
Making a sense of volume by expressing overlapping parts.

同色の色鉛筆でデニムの綾織りを斜線で入れます。
Drawing the twill weaving of denim by adding diagonal lines with the colored pencil of the same color.

使用画材［ガッシュ・色鉛筆・アルシュ紙（細目）］
Materials Used [Gouache · Colored pencil · ARCHES (FINE)]

marker

マーカーで描く

Drawing with Marker

マーカーについて

　速乾性で濁りのない鮮明な発色が美しく、透明度が高いので色を重ねて混色しても彩度が下がらずスピード感あるタッチに仕上げることができます。また他のさまざまな画材と組み合わせて使えるため、幅広く活用できます。

About the Marker
The Marker is able to make the coloring with a sense of speed without losing its saturation even if the colors are mixed with layering on top. It has a fast-drying, a high degree of transparency and a clear color without turbidity, and produces beautiful color. In addition, it can be widely used because there is no problem to use in combination with various other painting tools/materials.

マーカーの種類　Type of the Markers

❶アルコール系油性マーカー：ペン先が太めのフェルトペンで紙への浸透が早く、カラーインクに近い濁りのない発色、重ね塗りしても下の色が透けます。混色はできないため、色鉛筆などと同じく色数が必要です。
＊カラーレスブレンダーで、ある程度グラデーション、ぼかしを表現することが可能です。

Alcohol type oil-based marker: It is a felt pen with a thick tip that has quick ink penetration to paper and clear color without turbidity similar to color ink. It shows the lower color even if it is overpainted. You need many colors as colored pencils because it is not capable with mixed color.
＊It is possible to express the gradation and blurring a little with a colorless blender.

❷水性顔料マーカー：油性マーカーのようににじむことなく描け、ストライプや細かい柄を描くのに適しています。ムラになりやすいので広い面を塗るのには適していません。

Aqueous pigment marker: It does not make a bleeding of ink as same as oil-based marker, and it is suitable for drawing stripes and fine patterns. It is not good for painting on a large surface as it can be uneven paint easily.

❸ドローイングペン：耐水性で美しい筆跡が特徴です。0.03ミリ～1.0ミリまでと筆跡幅もあり、アウトラインを入れるのに適しています。濃度も高く、乾燥性にもすぐれています。

Drawing pen: It has water resistance and beautiful brushstroke as characteristics. There are also various line width from 0.03 mm to 1.0 mm that are suitable for putting outlines. It has high density and excellent dryness.

❹筆ペン：墨を摺ることなく毛筆で強弱のある線が描けます。にじみ・かすれ等の工夫により、独特の味わいを持ったイラストを描くことができます。水彩と併せて使用する場合は、乾くと耐水性になるものを選びます。

Brush pen: It is able to draw strong and weak lines by brush tip without dissolving an Indian ink stick. It is possible to draw illustrations with unique taste by devising blurring and scratching effect. It is better to use a water resistant type that is able to be a waterproof after it gets dry, if you use it combining with watercolor.

❺水性顔料系ゲルインク：鮮やかで濃くにじまないのでストライプやチェック等の細かい柄を描くのに便利です。

Aqueous pigment gel ink: It is useful for drawing fine patterns such as stripes and plaids, because it makes vivid and strong color without blurring.

ドローイングペンの筆跡幅　Tip width of the Drawing pen

0.03mm	
0.05mm	
0.1mm	
0.3mm	
0.5mm	
0.8mm	
1.0mm	

●コピックスケッチ（ニブの形状）スーパーブラシ＆ミディアムブロード
ここで紹介しているのは穂先に腰があり使い勝手の良いスーパーブラシと角のあるミディアムブロードの組合わせですが、ニブの形状は他にも数種類あります。

Copic sketch (The shape of nibs) Super Brush & Medium Broad
Here, it shows one of Copic type that has a combination of a comfortable Super Brush that has resilient tip and a Medium Broad with angled tips, but there are some more variations for the shapes of nib.

カラーレスブレンダー
無色のインクが入っている溶剤マーカーで、ある程度グラデーションやぼかしを表現することが可能です。

Colorless Blender
It is a colorless ink marker that is able to express some gradation and blurring

注意）速乾性のためムラになりやすい
重ね塗りすることである程度ムラを抑えられますが、重ねることに色が濃くなります。重ねることも考えて、イメージより一段薄い色で塗ると良い。イメージの色、イメージより一段薄い色、イメージより1段濃い色と3本用意することでムラなく立体感のある塗り方ができます。用紙の種類や色によってムラになりやすいものがあるので、必ず、同じ用紙で試し塗りをします。

Attention) It is easy to be uneven paint because of quick drying.
It is possible to prevent unevenness to some extent by overpainting, but the color gets darker and darker with each time of overpainting. It is better to paint in color that is one step lighter than you imagine when you consider overpainting. Therefore, it is possible to color three-dimensionally without unevenness by preparing three color-variations such as an imagined color, the one step lighter color and the darker one. As some paper types and colors are easy to get unevenness, be sure to try on the same paper.

125

Give Coloring

濃・中・淡で立体感を出す *Creating a three-dimensional effect with shade in dark, medium and light*

3 一番明るい部分を残しながら一段明るくした中間の色で塗ります。
Applying the medium color that is brightened one step while leaving the brightest part.

1 肌を塗る時は頬紅を先に濃い色で塗り、薄い肌色で上から何回か塗り重ねると肌になじんで自然な感じに仕上がります。
At the time of applying the color on the skin, applying blusher first by dark color, and applying light skin color several times on the top to blend right in with the skin and finishing it natural.

2 濃い色でコートの影になる部分を塗ります。
Applying a dark color to the part of shadow for a coat.

4 薄い色のスーパーブラシで何回かなじませるように塗り重ねて全体を塗ります。
Overpainting a light color to the whole part several times by Super Brush as to blend right in with it.

126

Materials Used [Drawing pen・Oil-based marker・Colored pencil・FABRIANO (FINE)]

■着色しよう

5 透けた素材が重なる部分は一段薄い色で塗ります。
Applying the color that is one step paler, to the overlapping areas of the transparent fabric/material.

6 軽いタッチでスカーフを着色します。
Applying the color to the scarf with a light touch.

7 最後に面相筆を使って白のガッシュでスカーフの柄とハイライトを入れて仕上げます。
Finishing by putting highlights and patterns of skirt with using finepoint brush and white gouache at the end.

8 ファーは毛足の流れや方向に沿って着色します。
Applying the color on the fur along the flow and direction of the hair.

9 ブーツは濃淡を強調して描くことで硬質感を表現します。
Expressing a sense of hardness by drawing with emphasis on shading for the boot.

Give Coloring

色を重ねてニットを描く　Drawing the Knit fabric by layering colors

❶リブの編み地を意識しながらアウトラインを描きます。
Drawing an outline while concerning about knitting construction of ribbed fabric.

❸一段薄い色でなじませながら塗り重ねます。
Overpainting the color that is one step paler, as to blend right in with the base color.

❹太軸のエッジを使ってニットの編み柄を描きます。(甘いエッジがニットの編み感を表現)
Drawing a knit pattern with using the edge of thick axis. (Loose edge expresses texture of knitting on the knitwear)

パンツのストライプ柄は布の地の目を意識しながら描きます。
Drawing the stripe pattern of the pants while concerning about the grain line of the fabric.

❷光の当たる部分を白く残し、く地の色を塗ります。
Applying the base color with leaving white for the part in the light.

■着色しよう

5 面相筆を使い白のガッシュで柄を描き入れます。
Drawing a pattern by using a fine-point brush and white gouache.

6 濃いグレーで影を入れます。
Adding shadows with dark gray.

7 白の色鉛筆で仕上げます。
Finishing with a white colored pencil

使用画材 ［ドローイングペン・油性マーカー・水性顔料マーカー・色鉛筆・ファブリアーノ紙（細目）］
Materials Used [Drawing pen · Oil-based marker · Aqueous pigment marker · Colored pencil · FABRIANO (FINE)]

129

Various Painting Tools

いろいろな画材で描く
Drawing with Various Painting Tools

いろいろな画材

スモーキーな透明感を出すなら水彩よりパステルの方が適し、クリアーな透明感なら水彩が適しているように、それぞれの持っている画材の特徴を知り、生かしながら組み合わせることで多様な表現が可能です。

ここで紹介されている以外の画材も多くあり、また画材として扱われていない物の中にも意外な効果が得られることもあります。失敗を恐れず試してほしいと思います。逆に失敗から新たな可能性が広がることがよくあります。

Various painting tools/materials
As pastel is more suitable for smoky transparent expression than watercolor and the watercolor is suitable for clear transparent expression, the way of expression can be spread variously by knowing, using and combining the characteristics of each material. There are many tools/materials other than the painting tools/materials that are introduced here. We hope that you try a lot without being afraid of mistakes because some of tools/materials that are not treated as painting tools/materials, can also have unexpected amazing effects. On the contrary, new possibilities often spread from failures as well.

画材　Painting tools/materials

絵を描くのに使用する画材は数限りなくあり、ここで紹介する画材はそのごく一部に過ぎませんが、いずれも身近で使いやすくデザイン、構造、色や柄、素材等を簡単に表現できるものが中心になっています。

There are limitless numbers of painting tools/materials used to draw pictures, and the painting tools/materials introduced here are only a small part of them. However they are all familiar and easy to use, and these main tools/materials can easily express designs, structures, colors, patterns, materials, etc.

❶パステル：指で塗るだけの基本的な技法が簡単で手軽に扱え、豊かな色数と軽快で繊細なタッチから深みのあるタッチまで幅広い表現ができます。ソフト、セミハード、ハード、の3タイプがありハードパステルは硬くて彩度が低く大胆に描くのに適し、逆にソフトは彩度が高く、もろいが伸びが良く繊細に描けます。
Pastel: It is possible to have a wide range of expression from light and delicate touch to deep touch as being treated easily by the basic technique that is painting with fingers. There are three types of soft, semi-hard and hard. The hard pastels are hard and have low saturation, so they are suitable for drawing boldly. On the other hand soft one is fragile, smooth and possible to draw delicately because it has high saturation.

❷色鉛筆：いつも使い慣れている鉛筆と、同じ感覚で手軽に扱える色鉛筆は、色が豊富で細かいところまで描け、他の画材とのなじみも良く、筆圧や方向、スピードを変えることで、バリエーションも広がり、また色を混ぜることによって多様な混色を楽しむことができます。
Colored pencil: It is possible to handle easily in the same way as a pencil that is used always. It is rich in color and possible to draw details, use combination with other paint tools/materials, and create many variations by changing pen pressure, direction, and speed. It is also possible to enjoy various mixed color by mixing colors.

❸水彩色鉛筆：普通に描いて、その上から水をつけた筆でなするとすぐに溶けだし水彩画のような感じになります。淡い水彩画の表現ができます。水につけなければ普通の色鉛筆と同じです。
Watercolor pencil: It is possible to draw as watercolor by melting, after you draw normally and trace by a brush that contains water on top. It can express pale watercolor paintings. It is the same as an ordinary colored pencil if it is not added water.

❹インク：濁りのない鮮明な発色性と抜群の透明性が特徴。水で薄めたり、混色することも可能で完全乾燥後に耐水性になるので、パステルや色鉛筆との相性も良く、組み合わせて描くことで深みが出ます。
Ink: It has excellent transparency and clear chromogenic property without turbidity. It can be diluted with water or mixed with other colors. It also works well with pastels and colored pencils because of getting water-resistant after being completely dried. Therefore, it produces richness and deepness by drawing in combination.

❺ドローイングペン：水性顔料インクで乾くと耐水性になりインク濃度も高く、ムラのないスムーズな筆跡はアウトラインを入れるのに適しています。
Drawing pen: It is the aqueous pigment ink and it becomes water resistant after it is dried. It is suitable for drawing outlines because it has high ink density and its brushstroke is smooth and evenly.

❻ボールペンゲルインク：絵の具の上から上塗りできるので細かい柄やシルバージップ、ゴールドボタンなどに使うと効果的です。
Ball-point pen with gel ink: It is effective to use it for fine patterns, silver zippers, gold buttons, etc. because it can be overpainted onto the paint.

❼筆ペン：強弱が簡単につけられる筆ペンは、仕上げのスミ入れやラフな柄入れが手軽にできます。
Brush pen: It can be easily controlled the strength of touch, is convenient to put a final touch or a rough pattern.

❽擦筆：パステル画などを擦ってぼかすのに使用します。特に細かい部分を塗るときに必要です。
Tortillon: It is used to blur the pastel drawing etc. by rubbing. It is necessary especially when you apply colors into the fine part.

131

■Give Coloring

ウォーム素材を描く *Drawing Warm materials/fabrics*

1 はじめに肌の色を塗り、充分に乾いてから、カッターナイフでソフトパステルの粉を一番濃くなるところに落とします。
First of all, applying the color of skin and dry sufficiently, then shaving soft pastel by using a cutter knife and putting the powder of it to the darkest color place.

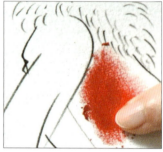

2 パステルの粉を指で擦りながらのばします。
Rubbing the pastel powder with fingers and spreading it.

3 濃くしたいところは強く、薄くしたいところは軽く調子をとりながら立体感を表現します。
Expressing a three-dimensional effect with controlling strength such as strongly rubbing to the place you want to make it darker, and lightly rubbing to the place you want to make it lighter.

パステルの粉が飛び散ると画面が汚れてしまうため、少しずつ調子を見ながら粉を落としていきます。塗った後の余分な粉は息を吹きかけて取り、はみ出した部分は練り消しゴムで拭き取ります。

Since the paper becomes dirty if the powder of the pastel is flying off, the powder needs to be placed while checking the amount little by little. Removing extra powder by blowing after painting and wiping off the wasted powder with a kneaded eraser.

フィクサチーフ（定着液）：パステルは手を触れると簡単に落ちてしまいます。このため完成後にフィクサチーフでパステルを定着させます。いきなり勢いよくかけると、しみになったり粉が吹き飛んで画面が汚れてしまうので、30cm位はなして全体に薄く均一に吹き付けましょう。
●色に深みを出したいときは、一度フィクサチーフで定着させ乾いたあとに再度塗り重ねます。

Fixatif (Liquid Fixative): Pastels fall off easily if somebody touches it. For this reason, preserve the pastels with the Fixatif after completion. It becomes stain or the powder is blown off to make the paper dirty, if it was applied vigorously too much.
●Overpainting it again after fixing with the fixatif and drying if you want to get some deepness in the color.

132

■着色しよう

4 鉛筆パステルを使って毛足を描き、深み
を出すため2色使いにします。
Drawing the hair of fur using pencil pastels. Expressing richness of color by using two colors.

5 擦筆（サッピツ）を使って内から外に毛
の流れに沿ってこすりながらぼかします。
Blurring by rubbing from the inside to the outside along the hair flow with using a pen (Tortillon).

6 白の色鉛筆で毛足のハイライトを描いて
衿を仕上げます。
Finishing the collar part by drawing the highlights on hair of fur with white colored pencils.

7 最後に白の鉛筆でハイライトを入れて仕
上げます。
Finishing by putting highlights with white colored pencils at the end.

8 パンツは黒と茶色の2色を直接塗り
重ねます。
Overpainting two colors of black and brown directly onto the pants.

使用画材［ソフトパステル・鉛筆パステル・色鉛筆・ファブリアーノ紙（細目）］
Materials Used [Soft pastel · Pencil pastel · Colored pencil · FABRIANO (FINE)]

133

■Give Coloring

レザーを描く *Drawing the Leather*

1 エスキースで確認します。
Confirming with Esquisse (rough sketches).

2 線を整理して墨入れし肌色を塗ります。
Organizing the lines, adding in ink and applying the color of skin.

3 鉛筆パステルで影になる濃い部分を塗ります。
Applying the dark color on the shadow part by pencil pastels.

4 光の当たる部分を残しながら擦筆（さっぴつ）で布地の方向に沿ってこすりなじませます。
Blending it well by rubbing with Tortillon along the direction of the fabric while leaving the part that is lighted.

5 全体の調子を見ながら足りないところを塗り足して素材感を強調します。
Emphasizing the texture by adding in the missing parts while checking the tone overall.

6 明るい部分を練り消しゴムを使って、色を抜き取ります。
Removing the color from the parts that is lighted by using a kneaded eraser.

134

■着色しよう

[7]練り消しゴムの先を細くして光沢感を強調したい部分をさらに拭き取ります。
Removing the color more from the parts that you want to emphasize a sense of luster by using a tip of kneaded eraser.

[8]顔料インクのシルバーペンでファスナーを描きます。
Drawing a zipper with a silver pen of the pigment ink.

[9]最後に白の色鉛筆で仕上げます。
Finishing with a white colored pencil at the end.

Q & A

濃くなりすぎて立体感が出なくなってしまった場合は？
What if the color gets dark too much and does not show a three-dimensional effect?

練り消しゴムで拭き取り、白のパステルで光の当たる部分を描き擦筆で擦る。白の色鉛筆で仕上げる。
Wiping off the color with a kneaded eraser and applying the color onto the part that is lighted with a white pastel and rubbing it with Tortillon. Finishing with a white colored pencil.

使用画材［鉛筆パステル・顔料インク・色鉛筆・ファブリアーノ紙（細目）］
Materials Used [Pencil pastel · Pigment ink · Colored pencil · FABRIANO (FINE)]

■Give Coloring

シャイニング素材を描く Drawing Shining materials/fabrics

マーカーは重ねて塗ると色が濃くなるため、肌色は薄めの色を選び、調子を見ながら塗り重ねます
Applying the color while confirming the tone by choosing lighter skin color first, because the color of the marker gets darker when it is overpainted.

影は濃く、光の当たる部分は薄く強弱をつけます
Adding darker shades on the shadow parts and lighter shades on the parts that is lighted.

光の当たる部分を多く表現することで軽さと光沢感を出します
Creating a sense of lightness and gloss by expressing a lot of parts that is lighted.

ポーズによる布地の動きに合わせて影を深く塗ります
Applying shadows stronger depending on the movement of fabric that is created by posing.

手軽なボールペン型の顔料インクで軽く滑るようにクロスハッチングを加えます
Adding cross-hatching lightly and smoothly with handy ball-point pen type pigment ink.

❶ドローイングペンで墨入れするときは、線が硬くならないように軽く滑るように描きます。
Drawing the lines lightly and smoothly with avoiding hard lines when you put inks by a drawing pen.

❷反射する光の強弱が複雑に出る光沢素材は、明暗をはっきりつけて地塗りします。
Applying the base paint with dividing light and dark clearly in case of drawing the glossy fabric/material that reflects the light intricately.

❸薄めの色で地塗りを加え顔料インクのボールペンで繊細な織感を描きます。
Drawing delicate weaving texture by a ball-point pen of pigment ink with adding light color on the base paint.

■着色しよう

求める光沢具合によって白の顔料インクのボールペンでクロスハッチングを加えて表現します
Expressing by adding cross-hatching with a ball-point pen type of white pigment ink, depending on the glossiness needed.

使用画材［マーカー・ゲルインクボールペン・アルシュ紙（細目）］
Materials Used [Marker · Ball-point pen with gel ink · ARCHES (FINE)]

④極細の面相筆を使い、白のガッシュでさらに織感を描き加えて織り糸の輝きを出します。
Expressing the shininess of yarn by adding more texture of weaving with using extra fine-pointed brush and white gouache.

⑤不透明なジンクホワイトで複雑な輝きを表現し、最後にダイヤモンド・ダストを入れて仕上げます。
Finishing by putting diamond dust at the end, with expressing complex shininess by using opaque Zinc White.

137

■Give Coloring

さまざまな画材の組み合わせ　*Combination of various painting tools/materials*

■アストラカン　*Astrakhan*

■1 たっぷりの水を引き丸筆で色をたらし、ゆっくりにじませます。
Putting plenty of water and applying the dark color by a round brush to bleed slowly.

■2 部分的に濃い色をおいて濃淡をつけます。
Adding shades by putting dark color on some parts.

■3 よく乾いたあと地塗りに添って濃淡をつけながらアストラカンまだら模様を描きます。
Drawing the unique mottled pattern of Astrakhan while adding shades along the base paint after it dried sufficiently.

■4 同色のパステルで毛羽立ち感を描き加えて仕上げます。
Finishing by adding a feeling of fuzz with pastel of the same color.

■クロコダイル　*Crocodile*

■1 目安となる型押しの線を軽く引きます。
Drawing the embossed pattern lightly as a guide.

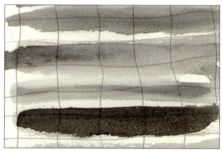

■2 光っているところを残して濃淡をつけます。
Adding shades while leaving the part that is lighted.

■3 クロコダイルのスケールを強調するように影の部分を濃く塗ります。
Applying the dark color on the shadow part as emphasizing the scales of crocodiles.

■4 全体のバランスを見ながら光沢、スケールの陰影を描いく仕上げます。
Finishing by drawing the gross and shades of scales while confirming the balance of overall.

■ 着色しよう

■ ニット Knit

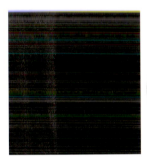

① ガッシュで濃いめにしっかりと地塗りをします。
Applying the dark color firmly as a base paint with using gouache.

② 色鉛筆を寝かせて軽く浮かせるように斜線を描きます。
Drawing diagonal lines by using colored pencil that is tilted and slightly floated.

③ 全体の調子を見ながら強弱をつけて描き加えます。ざらざらした表面感が一度編んだ糸をほどき、再度編み立てたニット・デ・ニットの素材感を引き出します。
Adding to draw with strength and weakness while confirming the tone overall. The rough texture makes the texture of knit-de-knit that is reknit fabric made by raveling and restructuring knit fabric once.

コートのアウトラインは薄く軽く描きます
Drawing the outline of the coat thinly and lightly.

厚みのあるコートを描く場合通常の素材よりボリュームが出るため、考えているより分量感をタップリもたせ丸みのあるラインで描きます
Drawing the line with roundness that has more volume than a sense of volume you think because the volume is larger than ordinary materials when you draw a coat with thickness.

使用画材［ガッシュ・油性マーカー・ソフトパステル・色鉛筆・マーメイド紙（細目）］
Materials Used [Gouache · Oil-based marker · Soft pastel · Colored pencil · MERMAID (FINE)]

■Give Coloring

ギャラリー・1 *Gallery・1*

使用画材　[割り箸・刷毛・墨汁・ガッシュ]
Materials Used [Wooden chopsticks・Brush・Indian ink・Gouache]

■着色しよう

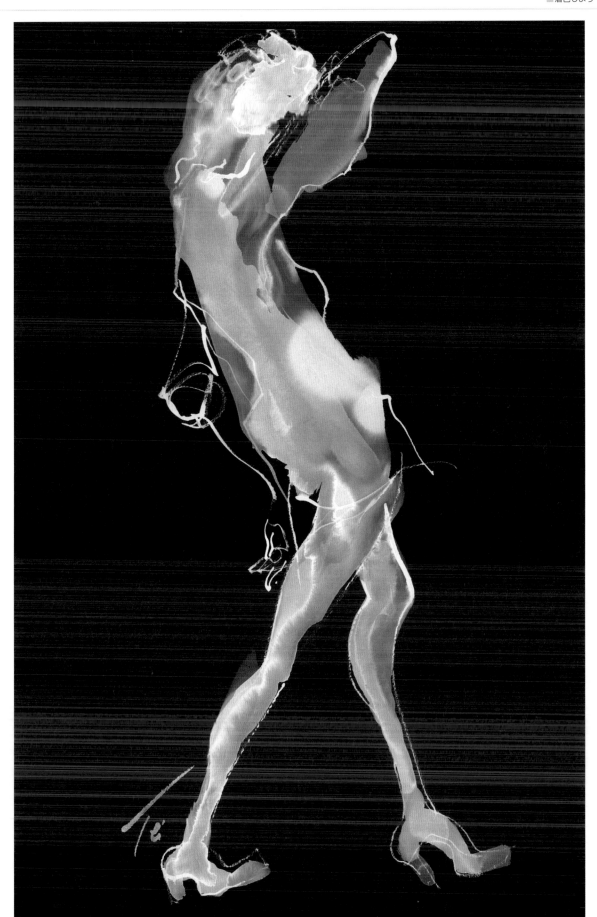

■Give Coloring

ギャラリー・2 *Gallery・2*

■着色しよう

使用画材 ［割り箸・刷毛・墨汁・ガッシュ］
Materials Used [Wooden chopsticks · Brush · Indian ink · Gouache]

143

第4章
フォトショップで描く

ファッションビジネスの現場で
データのプレゼンテーションが
常識となっている現在
デザイン提案や個性的な企画書を作成するには
Photoshopは欠かすことのできないツールです。
この章では、素材表現やデザイン画、
企画マップの作成の仕方を、より実践的理解を
深めるために下記「URL」からダウンロードして
Photoshopの基本をマスターします。
▶ https://www.tei-619.com/download

Chapter 4
Drawing with Photoshop

Presentations with digital data have become a common sense approach in the field of fashion business, and Photoshop is now an indispensable tool to create a design proposal and business plan of great originality. In this chapter, you are going to master basics of Photoshop by downloading textures, design illustrations and design proposal illustrations from the following URL to deepen practical understanding.
▶ *https://www.tei-619.com/download*

145

■Do Photoshop

色について *Colors*

1）RGBカラーとCMYKカラー　*RGB color model and CMYK color model*

　モニターなどに見られる色光の三原色は、R（レッド）G（グリーン）B（ブルーバイオレット）に色を混ぜるほど明度が上がり、白に近づくので加法混色と言われています。
　対して印刷などに見られる色料の三原色は、C（シアン）M（マゼンタ）Y（イエロー）に色を混ぜるほど明度が下がり黒に近づくので減法混色と言われています。プロセスカラー印刷では、黒の部分を引き締めるためにB（ブラック）を追加してCMYKの4色で最終的な色を表現しています。

The primary additive colors displayed in screens are called "additive mixture", because the more red, green and blue violet are mixed, the whiter the result is with higher brightness. On the other hand, the subtractive primary colors are used for subtractive mixture, because the more cyan, magenta and yellow are mixed, the darker the result is with lower brightness. Process color printing prints with CMYK, representing the three colors above and black added to print refined black.

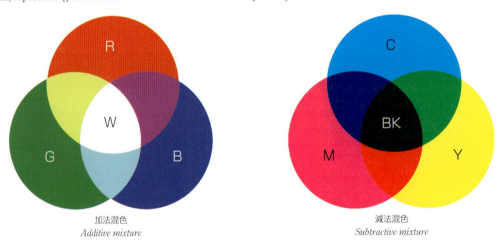

加法混色
Additive mixture

減法混色
Subtractive mixture

2）CMYKの12色相環をベースに色をつくる　*Creating a color from a CMYK color wheel*

　CMYKのうち、1色または2色をそれぞれ100％ずつまたは、片方を50％混ぜた色だけで12個の色相環ができます。これらはプロセスカラーの原理上、それぞれの色相において最も彩度が高い色（純色）となります。

A 12 color wheel contains cian, mazenta, yellow, and other colors created by mixing two colors selected from the three in equal amounts and in a two-to-one ratio. As a principle of process color, each of these 12 colors is the most saturated color (purest color) of their individual hue category.

色を決めていくとき、まず純色での色味を選び「明るさ」「彩度」の順に操作すると複雑な色も出しやすくなります。

You can easily create a delicate color by choosing firstly a color from the purest colors to change secondly its brightness and saturation.

146

3) Photoshopでカラーを選択する方法 *How to select a color in Photoshop*

色の選択方法はいくつかあります。スポイトツール、カラーパネル、スウォッチパネルまたはカラーピッカーを使用して、新しい描画色や背景色を指定することができます。

There are multiple ways to select a color. You can select a new foreground or background color using the Eye Dropper tool, the Color panel, the Swatches panel or the Adobe Color Picker.

❶ツールパネルの描画色と背景色のカラー 選択ボックス
  A. 描画色と背景色を初期設定に戻すアイコン
  B. 描画色と背景色を入れ替えアイコン
  C. 描画色カラー選択ボックス
  D. 背景色カラー選択ボックス

1. The Foreground and Background color boxes in the Tools panel
  A. Default colors icon
  B. Switch colors icon
  C. Foreground color box
  D. Background color box

A. 描画色と背景色を初期設定に戻すアイコン *Default colors icon*
B. 描画色と背景色を入れ替えるアイコン *Switch colors icon*
C. 描画色カラー選択ボックス *Foreground color box*
D. 背景色カラー選択ボックス *Background color box*

❷スポイトツールによるカラーの選択
  スポイトツールは、カラーをサンプルして新しい描画色または背景色を指定します。カラーは、アクティブな画像または画面上の任意の場所からサンプルすることができます。

2. Selecting a color with the Eye Dropper tool
  The Eye Dropper tool samples a color to select a new foreground or background color. You can sample from the active image or from anywhere else on the screen.

スポイトツール *The Eye Dropper tool*

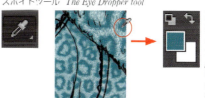

スポイトの先を抽出したいカラーの上でクリックすると描画色に反映される。
You can select a new foreground color by positioning the tip of the eyedropper over the color you want to sample to and clicking it.

❸カラーピッカーによるカラーの選択
  描画色をクリックするとカラーピッカーが表示されます。「HSB」「RGB」および「Lab」テキストボックスにカラー値を入力するか、カラースライダーまたはカラーフィールドを使用することによって、カラーを選択できます。

3. Selecting a color with the Color Picker
  You can choose a color by clicking the foreground color to open the Color Picker. You can enter color component values in the HSB, RGB and Lab text boxes, or using the color slider or the color field.

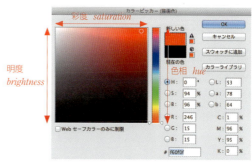

彩度 *saturation*
明度 *brightness*
色相 *hue*

Photoshopのカラーピッカー。色相と明度、彩度の3つの属性をそれぞれ独立して操作することで色を決めることができます。
Color Picker in Photoshop. You can select a color by setting separately the three properties: hue, saturation and brightness.

❹スウォッチパネルによるカラーの選択と追加および削除
  カーソルをスウォッチパネル上に移動させるとスポイトツールになります。選択したいカラーの上にスポイトの先を合わせてクリックすると描画色に反映されます。

4. Selecting, adding and deleting a color in the Swatches panel
  When you position the cursor on the Swatches panel, it turns into the Eye Dropper tool. You can select a new foreground color by positioning the tip of the eyedropper on the color you want to select and clicking it.

❺カラーパネルによるカラーの選択
  カラーパネル（ウィンドウ／カラー）には、現在の描画色および背景色のカラー値が表示されます。カラーパネルのスライダーを使用して、異なるカラーモデルで描画色および背景色を編集できます。

5. Selecting a color in the Color panel
  The Color panel (Window / Color) displays the color values for the current foreground and background colors. Using the sliders in the Color panel, you can select a new foreground and background colors in a different color model.

スウォッチパネル *The Swatches panel*

スウォッチパネルへのカラーの追加
1. 追加するカラーを指定し、描画色にします。
2. 次のいずれかの操作を行います。
スウォッチパネルの新規スウォッチボタンをクリックします。または、スウォッチパネルメニュー から「新規スウォッチ」を選択します。

Adding a color to the Swatches panel
1. Change the foreground color to the color you want to add to the Swatches panel.
2. Do one of the following:
Click the New Swatch button in the Swatches panel. Alternatively, choose New Swatch from the Swatches panel menu.

カラーパネル *Color panel*

描画色 *Foreground color*
背景色 *Background color*
スライダー *Slider*
カラーランプ *Color ramp*

カラーの選択時に次の警告がカラーパネルに表示される場合もあります。
The Color panel may display an alert when you select a color.

■Do Photoshop

Photoshopのツールパネル Tools Panel in Photoshop

　ツールパネルは画像を加工するためのさまざまなツールを選択するための特殊なウィンドウのことです。ツールボックスに表示されているアイコンをクリックすると、ツールを選択することができます。
Tools panel is a special window to select various tools to edit an image. You can select a tool by clicking its icon displayed in the Tools panel.

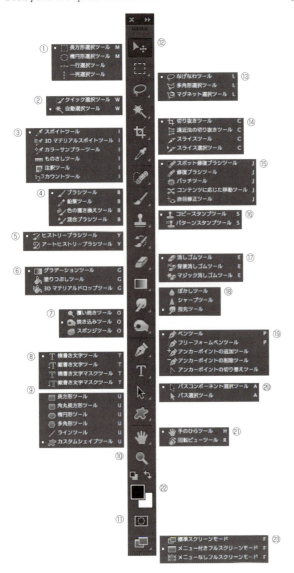

⑥グラデーションツール：グラデーションを描画します。
Gradient tool: makes a gradient.

⑦覆い焼きツール：ドラッグした部分を明るくします。
Dodge tool: lightens an area which you drag over.

⑧テキストツール：フォント・サイズ・カラーなどの書式設定を行います。
Type tool: is used for formatting text and specifying style, size and color of font.

⑨長方形ツール：長方形や楕円形などの図形描画ツールは総称して「ベクトルシェイプツール」または「シェイプツール」と呼ばれています。
Rectangle tool: Tools to draw rectangles, ellipses and other shapes are collectively called Vector Shape tool or Shape tool.

⑩ズームツール：画像の表示倍率を変更します。
Zoom tool: changes the display magnificaiton of an image.

⑪クイックマスクモード：画像の描画モードを指定します。クイックマスクでは、画像に一時的なマスクができます。
Quick Mask Mode: specifies the blending mode of an image. The Quick Mask creates a temporary mask for an image.

⑫移動ツール（ショートカット：V）：選択範囲やレイヤーをドラッグして移動するときに使います。
Move tool (Shortcut: V): Drags and moves a selection area and layer.

⑬なげなわツール：自由な形の選択範囲や、輪郭検出できる選択機能を利用したいときに使います。
Lasso tool: makes a freeform selection or detects automatically an outline.

⑭切り抜きツール：画像の一部だけを、四角く切り抜くことができます。
Crop tool: removes square portions of an image.

⑮修復ブラシツール／パッチツール：しわやゴミなどを自動的に消したり、きれいにしてくれるツールです。
Refine brush tool/Patch tool: delete or reduce easily wrinkles and dust.

⑯スタンプツール：背景の調子を整えたい時などに、指定したコピー元からコピー先へと、画像をコピーするときに使います。
Stamp tool: samples pixels of an area of an image to paint the area on another image, which is useful to adjust the background.

⑰消しゴムツール：画像を消したいときはドラッグして消します。
Eraser tool: erases part of an image you drag over.

⑱ぼかしツール：ドラッグした部分をぼかします。ほかに、画像をシャープにするシャープツールや、画像をなじませる指先ツールがあります。
Blur tool: blurs an area you drag over. It can be expanded to show the Sharp tool and Smudge tool which sharpen and soften an image, respectively.

⑲ペンツール：「パスオブジェクト」や「シェイプ」を描くためのツールです。
Pen tool: draws "Path object" or "Shape".

⑳パスコンポーネント選択ツール：パスで構成された図形をワンクリックで選択し移動や削除などの編集をすばやく行います。
Path component selection tool: selects a shape which consists of paths with a single-click to move, delete and edit it with speed.

㉑手のひらツール：画像をドラッグして、ドキュメントウィンドウに表示されていない範囲を表示します。
Hand tool: drags an image to bring its hidden area into the document window.

㉒描画色と背景色：描画色（左）背景色（右）を指定できます。右上の矢印で描画色と背景色を入れ替え、左上の黒白四角で初期化（描画色：黒、背景色：白）にします。
Foreground and Background color: select the foreground color (the left color) and background color (the right color). The arrow above the right side switches the foreground and background color, and the black and white squares above the left side restore the default foreground and background colors (The foreground and background color are black and white in the default settings, respectively).

㉓スクリーンモード：Photoshopの作業エリアの表示状態を切り替えます。
Screen mode: switches the display state of the workspace.

①選択範囲ツール：四角形や楕円形など、ある決まった形の選択範囲を作成するときに使います。
Marquee tool: is used to make a rectangular, elliptical, and other shape selection area.

②自動選択ツール：クリックしたピクセルの近似色を判断して自動的に選択範囲を作成します。
Magic Wand tool: makes a selection area automatically outlined by detecting similar colors to the color of the pixel you click.

③スポイトツール：クリックした位置の色の情報を取得します。
Eyedropper tool: gets properties of the color of a point you click.

④ブラシツール：選択している描画色で画像上をドラッグして描画します。
Brush tool: is used for painting the foreground color over an image by dragging over it.

⑤ヒストリーブラシツール：ヒストリー機能で得られた画像をブラシにします。
History Brush tool: creates a brush tip shape by sampling pixels of an image in the history panel.

148

■フォトショップで描く

Photoshopのパネル　*Other Panels in Photoshop*

　画像の修正や変更、確認を行う時に操作します。パネルは必要に応じて小さくしたり、隠したり、他のパネルとまとめて整理することもできます。

You can use these panels to edit an image and view its information. The tools panel can be reduced, hidden and grouped with other panels.

①

②

③

④

⑤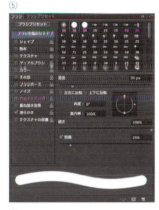

⑥

⑦

⑧

⑨

⑩

①カラーパネル：描画色および背景色のカラー値が表示されます。
Color panel: displays the color values for the foreground and background colors.

②スウォッチパネル：スウォッチとは、カラーや濃度（色合い）、グラデーション、パターンに名前を付けたものです。よく使用するカラーを格納します。スウォッチパネルでは、カラーを追加または削除したり、プロジェクト別に異なるカラーのライブラリを表示することができます。
Swatches panel: "Swatch" means a small piece named in accordance with its color, density, gradient or pattern. The Swatches panel stores colors frequently used. In this panel, you can add and delete a color, and display different color libraries separately made for each project.

③色調補正パネル：元の画像を壊すことなく画像補正ができます。トーンカーブ、レベル補正、色彩・彩度などさまざまな色調補正が1つのインターフェイスから編集が可能。すべての編集が自動的に調整レイヤーとして適用されます。
Color Adjustments panel: adjusts image properties without destroying the original image. You can select Curves, Levels, Hue/Saturation and other color adjustments in this panel and applying any of these adjustments automatically create an adjustment layer.

④スタイルパネル：ドロップシャドウやベベルなどの視覚効果をレイヤー上のオブジェクトに適用する「レイヤースタイル」を、文字やシェイプ、画像のレイヤーに適用することができます。
Styles panel: applies a layer style adding visual effects like Drop Shadow or Bebel to characters, shapes, images and other objects on a layer.

⑤ブラシ／ブラシプリセット：ブラシのプリセットは、サイズ、シェイプ、硬さなどの特性が定義された保存済みのブラシ先端です。プリセットブラシは、よく使用する特性と共に保存することができます。
Brush/Brush Settings: The Brush Settings are brush tips saved with defined size, shape, hardness and other properties. You can save a brush setting with brush properties you select often.

⑥レイヤーパネル：Photoshopのレイヤーは、積み重ねられた透明フィルムのようなものです。レイヤーの透明部分では、下のレイヤーが透けて見えます。また、レイヤーの不透明度を変更して、コンテンツを部分的に透明にすることもできます。
Layers panel: Layers in Photoshop are like sheets of stacked acetate. You can see through transparent areas of a layer to the layers below. You can also change the opacity of a layer to make content partially transparent.

⑦チャンネル／パス：チャンネルは、さまざまな種類の情報を保存するグレースケール画像です。
Channels/paths: Channels are grayscale images that store different types of information.

⑧ヒストリーパネル：操作の取り消しや、やり直しをすることができます。画像のピクセルに変更を加えるたびに、その画像の新規のヒストリー画像がヒストリーパネルに追加されます。それぞれの処理を行った後の状態が別々のヒストリー画像としてパネルに表示されます。
History panel: Allows you to undo and redo an operation. Each time you apply a change to pixels of an image, a new history thumbnail of the changed image is added to the panel. The panel displays history thumbnails showing states after each process.

⑨文字パネル：カーニング、字送り、ベースラインシフトおよびテキストのスケールを行うことができます。
Character panel: allows you to set Kerning, Tracking, Baseline Shift and to scale text.

⑩属性：各種レイヤーに設定された「属性」を表示するパネルです。
Properties panel: displays properties of various layers.

149

Do Photoshop

Photoshopの画面と名称　Workspace in Photoshop and Names of its Elements

1) ツールパネルとその他のパネル　Tools panel and other panels

　Photoshopの新規画像を開くとこのような画面になっています。各種メニューを納めた「メニューバー」が一番上にあり、二段目に各ツール機能のオプションが表示される「オプションバー」があります。右端にはパネル類、左端に作業に使うツール類がまとめられた「ツールパネル」があります。基本の名称と機能を覚えておきましょう。

This screen appears when you open a new image in Photoshop. The menu bar shows various menues at the top, and the Options bar is in the second row displaying options of each tool function. The Tools panel shows various tools on the left side and other panels are located on the right side. Let us learn their name and basic functions.

メニューバー：「ファイルを開く」「補正機能を呼び出す」など各種の機能を呼び出す一覧です。
Menu bar: is a list to choose Open, Adjustments, and other various commands.

オプションバー：ツールパネルで選んでいるツールに合わせて表示が変わりツールごとの詳細な設定（オプション項目）を変更できます。
Options bar: displays specific settings of the tool selected in the Tools panel and allows you to change them (optional entries).

ヒストリー：操作の内容を記録し、簡単に操作を前の状態に戻して途中から再度やり直すことができます。
History: saves your operation contents and allow you to undo your operations and redo your work.

カラー／スウォッチ：描画色や背景色を指定します。
Colors/Swatches: select the foreground color and background color.

色調補正：色調補正の機能をアイコンで選択することで自動的にそのモードにパネルが切り替わり調整レイヤーができます。
Color adjustment: displays automatically an adjustment panel and creates an adjustment layer in accordance with a color adujstment icon you selected.

ツールパネル：画像を編集するための基本的なツールが格納されている道具箱です。
Tools panel: is a box containing basic tools to edit an image.

レイヤー／チャンネル／パス：レイヤーの状態を表示したり、各種レイヤーの新規作成や削除、移動などが行えます。
Layers/Channels/paths: display a layer state and allow you to create, delete and move multiple types of layers.

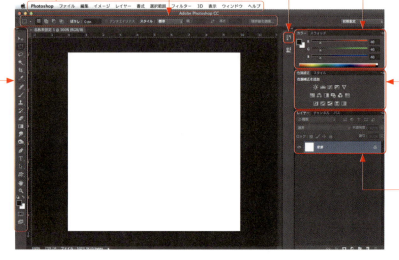

2) 新規書類　New document

　メニューバー「ファイル」から「新規」を実行すると「新規ドキュメント」が表示されます。ここで任意のサイズを作成します。カスタムでは、「用紙のサイズ」「解像度」「カラーモード」などが指示できます。

You can open the New Document dialog box by choosing New in the File menu. Any size of the document can be selected in this dialog box. You can also select a Custom item to specify the document size, resolution, color mode and other details.

用紙のサイズ（幅、高さ）
Document Size (width, height)

解像度
Resolution

カラーモード
Color Mode

150

フィルターで素材づくり
Creating Textures with Filters

■Do Photoshop

フィルターで作る凹凸素材とウオッシュデニム
Creating a Rough Texture and Washed Denim Texture with Filters

　フィルターは、画像にさまざまな効果を与えるために使われます。画像を絵画的にしたり、変形したり逆光を描画するなど数多くあります。またフィルターを組み合わせることで、複雑な効果を得ることもできます。

Filters add many various effects to an image, such as hand-painted effect, distortion, or backlight effect.
You can also combine filters to create more delicate effects.

1) ワッフル調やブークレ、バスケット織など凹凸のある素材
Creating Waffle Fabric, Boucl, Basket Weave and Other Rough Fabric Textures

　色の選択方法はいくつかあります。スポイトツール、カラーパネル、スウォッチパネルまたはカラーピッカーを使用して、新しい描画色や背景色を指定することができます。

There are multiple ways to select a color. You can select a new foreground or background color using the Eye Dropper tool, the Color panel, the Swatches panel or the Adobe Color Picker.

❶メニューバー「ファイル」から「新規」を選択し新規書類を作成します。
　◆「ファイル名」をダブルクリックし、名前を記入します。
　◆書類のサイズ／幅10cm×高さ10cm
　◆解像度／150pixel/inch
　◆カラーモード／RGBカラー
　◆カンバスカラー／白

1. In the File menu, choose New to create a new document.
　◆Double-click the Name to enter a file name.
　◆Document Size/10cm in width and 10cm in height
　◆Resolution/150 Pixels/Inch
　◆Color Mode/RGB color
　◆Background Contents/White

❷メニューバー「フィルター」から「フィルターギャラリー」を選択します。
2. In the Filter menu, choose Filter Gallery.

❸「フィルターギャラリー」の「テクスチャー」「クラッキング」を選択し、オプションからプレビュー画面で確認しながら数値設定します。
　◆溝の間隔／30
　◆溝の深さ／5
　◆溝の明るさ／6
　「OK」ボタンをクリックで完成です。

3. In the Filter Gallery menu, choose Texture > Craquelure and set the values in the panel until the preview shows the desired result.
　◆Crack Spacing/30
　◆Crack Depth/5
　◆Crack Brightness/6
　Click OK to complete the filter.

❹「フィルターギャラリー」の「テクスチャー」「モザイクタイル」を選択し、オプションからプレビュー画面で確認しながら数値設定します。
　◆タイルサイズ／23
　◆溝の幅／3
　◆溝の明るさ／6
　「OK」ボタンをクリックで完成です。

4. In the Filter Gallery menu, choose Texture > Mosaic Tiles and set the values in the panel until the preview shows the desired result.
　◆Tile size/23
　◆Grout Width/3
　◆Lighten Grout/6
　Click OK to complete the filter.

フィルターギャラリー「テクスチャ」から他にも「テクスチャライザー」や「パッチワーク」などイメージに合わせて試してみましょう。

In the Filter Gallery menu, let us try Texture > Texturizer, Patchwork and other filters for the desired result.

❶
◆ファイル名記入
◆書類のサイズ／幅10cm×高さ10cm
◆解像度／150pixel/inch
◆カラーモード／RGBカラー
◆カンバスカラー／白

◆Enter a file name.
◆Document Size／
　10cm in width and 10cm in height
◆Resolution/150 Pixels/Inch
◆Color Mode/RGB color
◆Background Contents/White

❷メニューバー「フィルター」から「フィルターギャラリー」を選択
In the Filter menu, choose Filter Gallery.

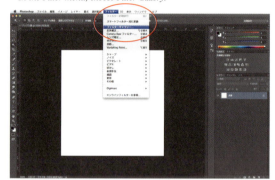

❸「クラッキング」
Craquelure

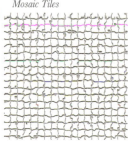

❹「モザイクタイル」
Mosaic Tiles

152

■フォトショップで描く

2) デニム調素材　*Denim texture*

❶ツールパネル「描画色」の色を選びます。（色の選択はP145を参照）

1. Click the foreground color in the Tools panel to select a new foreground color (See p.145 for color selection).

❷ツールパネル「塗りつぶしツール」を選択し画面の上でクリックして、描画色で塗りつぶします。

2. Choose the Paint Bucket tool and click the layer to fill it with the foreground color.

❸メニューバー「フィルター」から「ノイズ」→ノイズを加える」を選びます。
- ◆量／26
- ◆分布方法／均等に分布
- ◆「グレースケールノイズ」にチェック

3. In the Filter menu, choose Noise > Add Noise.
- ◆*Amount/26*
- ◆*Distribution/Uniform*
- ◆*Check the Monochromatic box.*

❹「フィルターギャラリー」の「アーティスティック」から「粗いパステル画」を選択しオプションでプレビュー画面で確認しながら数値設定します。
- ◆ストロークの長さ／40
- ◆ストロークの正確さ／20
- ◆テクスチャー／カンバス
- ◆拡大縮小／200％
- ◆レリーフ／50
- ◆照射方向／下へ

「OK」ボタンをクリックで完成です。

4. In the Filter Gallery, choose Artistic > Rough Pastels and set the values until the preview shows the desired result.
- ◆*Stroke Length/40*
- ◆*Stroke Detail/20*
- ◆*Texture/Canvas*
- ◆*Scaling/200%*
- ◆*Relief/50*
- ◆*Light/Top*

Click OK to finish the filter.

※数値によって表情が大きく変化します。イメージに合わせて数値を変えてみて下さい。

The result greatly changes in accordance with the values. Try different values for the desired result.

❶描画色
Foreground color

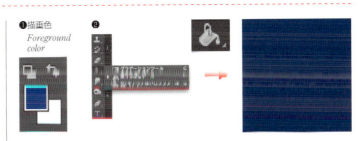

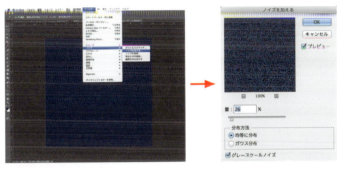

◆ストロークの長さ／19
◆ストロークの正確さ／6
◆*Stroke Length/19*
◆*Stroke Detail/6*

3) ウオッシュ感のあるデニム　*Washed denim texture*

❶ツールパネル「描画色」の色を選びます。

1. Click the foreground color in the Tools panel and select a new foreground color.

❷メニューバー「フィルター」から「描画」→「雲模様1」を選択します。

2. In the Filter menu, choose Render > Clouds 1.

◆「背景色」にも色が入ると描画色と背景色との混色で雲模様が表現されます。

You can also select a new background color to paint the white areas of cloud texture in the new background color.

◆背景色／白
◆*Background color/White*

◆背景色／色
◆*Background color/Another color*

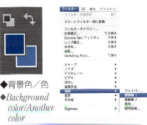

153

■ Do Photoshop

フィルターで作るボーダー、ストライプ、チェック
Creating Stripe and Check Patterns with Filters

1) ハーフトーンパターンでボーダーを作る　Creating a horizontal stripes pattern using Halftone Pattern

❶メニューバー「ファイル」から「新規」を選択し新規書類を作成します。
　◆「ファイル名」をダブルクリックし、名前を記入します。
　◆書類のサイズ／幅10cm×高さ10cm
　◆解像度／150pixel/inch
　◆カラーモード／RGBカラー
　◆キャンバスカラー／白

1. In the File menu, choose New to create a new document.
　◆Double-click the Name to enter a file name.
　◆Document Size/10cm in width and 10cm in height
　◆Resolution/150 Pixels/Inch
　◆Color Mode/RGB color
　◆Background Contents/White

❷「ツールパネル」で描画色を選択します。「カラー」R（レッド）／255
2. Select a foreground color in the Tools panel. Color: R/255

❸メニューバー「フィルターギャラリー」を開き「スケッチ」→「ハーフトーンパターン」を選びます。
3. In the Filter Gallery menu, choose Sketch > Halftone Pattern.

❹「ハーフトーンパターン」のオプションで数値設定します。
　◆サイズ／9
　◆コントラスト／50
　◆ハーフトーンパターン／線
「OK」ボタンクリックでボーダー完成です。

4. Set the values in the option of Halftone Pattern.
　◆Size/9
　◆Contrast/50
　◆Halftone Pattern/Strokes
Click OK to complete the filter.

❶

◆ファイル名記入
◆書類のサイズ／幅10cm×高さ10cm
◆解像度／150pixel/inch
◆カラーモード／RGBカラー
◆キャンバスカラー／白

◆Enter a file name.
◆Document Size/
　10cm in width and 10cm in height
◆Resolution/150 Pixels/Inch
◆Color Mode/RGB color
◆Background Contents/White

❷

❸ ❹

◆サイズ／9
◆コントラスト／50
◆ハーフトーンパターン／線
◆Size/9
◆Contrast/50
◆Halftone Pattern/Strokes

2) 2色ボーダー　Creating a horizontal stripes pattern with two colors

❶ツールパネル「描画色／背景色」の色を選択します。
1. Select a new foreground and background color in the Tools panel.

❷メニューバー「フィルターギャラリー」を開き「スケッチ」→「ハーフトーンパターン」を選びます。
2. In the Filter Gallery menu, choose Sketch > Halftone Pattern.

❸「ハーフトーンパターン」のオプションで数値設定します。
　◆サイズ／9
　◆コントラスト／0
　◆ハーフトーンパターン／線
3. Set the values in the opition of Halftone Pattern.
　◆Size/9
　◆Contrast/0
　◆Halftone Pattern/Strokes

❹オプションの数値のサイズを「1」に設定でピンストライプボーダーになります。
4. You can create a horizontal pin-stripes texture by setting the value of Size to 1.

❶ ❷

❹
◆サイズ／1
◆コントラスト／50
◆ハーフトーンパターン／線
◆Size/1
◆Contrast/50
◆Halftone Pattern/Strokes

❸
◆サイズ／9
◆コントラスト／0
◆ハーフトーンパターン／線
◆Size/9
◆Contrast/0
◆Halftone Pattern/Strokes

◆コントラストを「0」に設定でニットボーダーの風合いになります。
You can set the value of the Contrast to 5 to create a horizontal stripes texture of knitwear.

◆サイズを「1」でピンストライプボーダー
You can create a horizontal pin-stripes texture by setting the value of the Size to 1.

154

3）ハーフトーンパターンでチェッカーフラッグ（市松模様）を作る
Creating a checkered flag pattern (Plaid pattern) with Halftone Pattern

❺「ハーフトーンパターン」の「パターンタイプ」を「点」に
設定します。
◆サイズ／12
◆コントラスト／50
◆ハーフトーンパターン／点
OKボタンクリックで市松模様（チェッカーフラッグ）の完
成です。

5. *In the Halftone Pattern panel, set the Pattern Type to Dot.*
   ◆*Size/12*
   ◆*Contrast/50*
   ◆*Halftone Pattern/Dot*
   Click OK to complete the checkered flag pattern (Plaid pattern).

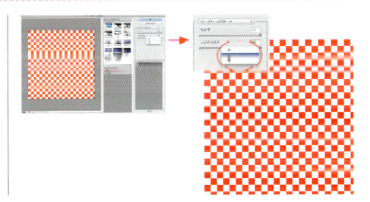

4）ハーフトーンパターン・レイヤー・描画モードでギンガムチェックを作る
Creating a gingham check with Halftone Pattern, two layers and the blending mode.

❶ハーフトーンパターンでボーダーを作成します。
  1. *Create a horizontal stripes pattern with Halftone Pattern.*

❷「レイヤーパネル」の「背景」レイヤーを右下の「新規レイ
ヤー作成」へドラッグします。
  2. *In the Layers panel, drag the background layer onto Create a New Document at the bottom right corner.*

❸「背景のコピー」レイヤーをメニューバー「編集」から「変形」
「90度回転」を選択し、回転させます。
  3. *In the Edit menu, choose Transform > Rotate 90° CW to rotate the "Background copy".*

❹「レイヤーパレット」の「不透明度」を60%に設定します。
ギンガムチェックのイメージに合わせて「不透明度」の数値
を設定します。
  4. *Set the opacity in the Layers panel to 60%.*
     You can try other values of the opacity to create the desired gingham check pattern.

❺フィルター「フィルターギャラリー」の「テクスチャー」「モザ
イクタイル」で凹凸のあるシアサッカータイプのテクスチャー
になります。
  5. *In the Filter Gallery menu, you can choose Texture > Mosaic Tiles to create a seersucker texture.*

❶

❷「新規レイヤー」へドラッグし「背景のコピー」を作成
Drag it onto Create a New Layer to create a "Background copy".

❸「編集」から「変形」「90度回転」でストライプ完成
In the Edit menu, choose Transform > Rotate 90° CW to complete the stripe pattern.

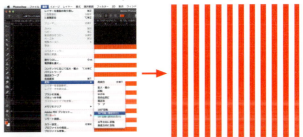

不透明度：60 *Opacity: 60*

回転させたレイヤー *Rotated layer*

❹不透明度の設定でギンガムチェック完成
Change the opacity to complete the gingham check pattern.

❺フィルタで凹凸のあるシアサッカー素材
Rough seersucker texture created with the filters.

■ Do Photoshop

フィルターと「グラデーション」で作る型押しパイソン
Creating a Python-Embossed Leather Texture Using Filters and Gradient

1) パイソン　Python-embossed leather texture

❶メニューバー「ファイル」から「新規」を選択し新規書類を作成します。
　◆「ファイル名」をダブルクリックし、名前を記入します。
　◆書類のサイズ／幅10cm×高さ10cm
　◆解像度／150pixel/inch
　◆カラーモード／RGBカラー
　◆カンバスカラー／白

1. In the File menu, choose New to create a new document.
　◆Double-click the Name to enter a file name.
　◆Document Size/10cm in width and 10cm in height
　◆Resolution/150 Pixels/Inch
　◆Color Mode/RGB color
　◆Background Contents/White

❷描画色を選択しメニューバー「編集」から「塗りつぶし」を選びます。

2. Select a new foreground color. Then click Fill in the Edit menu.

❸レイヤーパネル「新規レイヤー作成」ボタンをクリックして「レイヤー1」を作成します。

3. Click Create a New Layer in the Layers panel to create a "Layer 1".

❹ツールボックス「グラデーションツール」を選択します。

4. Choose the Gradient tool in the Tools panel.

❺オプションバー▼印をクリックして「グラデーションプリセット」を表示し、「イエロー、紫、オレンジ、青」を選択します。

5. Click the triangle in the Options bar to open the gradient presets and select the "Yellow, Violet, Orange, Blue".

❻グラデーションタイプの中から「線形グラデーションツール」を選びます。

6. Choose Linear Gradient from the gradient types icons.

❼上から下に向かってドラッグします。

7. Drag from the top to the bottom.

❽メニューバー「フィルター→ステンドグラス」を選択します。
　◆セルの大きさ／12
　◆境界線の太さ／6
　◆明るさの強さ／0
　※数値によってサイズが大きく変わるのでイメージに合わせて設定して下さい。

8. In the Filter menu, choose Stained Glass.
　◆Cell Size/12
　◆Border Thickness/6
　◆Light Intensity/0
　The cell size greatly changes in accordance with the value, so try different values for the desired result.

❾ツールパネル「自動選択ツール」で線の部分を選択します。(境界線の太さによって全ての線が選択されない場合、メニューバー「選択範囲→近似色を選択」で線の部分が全て選択されます。)

9. Select the border with the Quick Selection tool in the Tools panel. When the border is thin, the Quick Selection tool sometimes cannot select the entire border. In such cases, choose Similar in the Selection menu to select the entire border.

❿deleteキーを押して選択部分を消去します。

10. Press the Delete key to delete the selection area.

❶
◆ファイル名記入
◆書類のサイズ／幅10cm×高さ10cm
◆解像度／150pixel/inch
◆カラーモード／RGBカラー
◆カンバスカラー／白

◆Enter a file name.
◆Document Size/
　10cm in width and 10cm in height
◆Resolution/150 Pixels/Inch
◆Color Mode/RGB color
◆Background Contents/White

❷描画色を選び「編集→塗りつぶし」で描画された背景
The background filled by selecting the background color and choosing Fill in the Edit menu.

❸「新規レイヤー作成」をクリック
Click Create a New Layer.

❹グラデーションツールを選択
Choose the Gradient tool.

❺▼印をクリックしてカラーパネルを表示「イエロー、紫、オレンジ、青」を選択
Click the triangle to open the Color panel. Select the "Yellow, Violet, Orange, Blue".

❻線形グラデーションツールを選択
Select the Linear Gradient.

 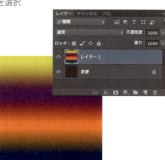

❼上から下にドラッグで描画
Drag from the top to the bottom to apply a gradient.

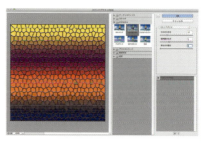

❽ステンドグラス
◆セルの大きさ／12
◆境界線の太さ／6
◆明るさの強さ／0

8. Stained Glass
◆Cell Size/12
◆Border Thickness/6
◆Light Intensity/0

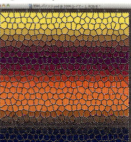

❾自動選択ツール
Quick Selection tool

■フォトショップで描く

⓫メニューバー「レイヤー→レイヤースタイル→ベベルとエンボス」を選びます。
11. In the Layer menu, choose Layer > Layer style > Bevel and Emboss.

⓬レイヤーパネルの「描画モード」を「オーバーレイ」に設定します。
12. In the Layers panel, set the blending mode to Overlay.

⓭レイヤーパネル「新規レイヤー作成」ボタンをクリックして「レイヤー2」を作成します。
13. In the Layers panel, click Create a New Layer to create a "Layer 2".

⓮メニューバー「編集」から「塗りつぶし」で塗りつぶします。
14. In the Edit menu, choose Fill to fill the layer.

⓯フィルターから「ノイズ→ノイズを加える」を選択し「グレースケールノイズ」にチェックを入れます。
◆量／90％
15. In the Filter menu, choose Noise > Add Noise and check the Monochromatic box.
◆*Amount/90%*

⓰フィルター「ピクセレート→水晶」を選びます。
◆セルの大きさ／42
16. In the Filter menu, choose Pixelate > Crystallize.
◆*Cell Size/42*

⓱フィルター「ぼかし→ぼかし（ガウス）」を選びます。
◆半径／6pixel
17. In the Filter menu, choose Blur > Gaussian Blur.
◆*Radius/6 pixels*

⓲レイヤーの「不透明度」を50％に設定し「描画モード」を「乗算」に設定します。
18. Set the opacity of the layer to 50% and the blending mode to Multiply.

⓫
◆スタイル／ベベル（内側）　◆高度／30
◆テクニック／滑らかに　◆ハイライトのモード／スクリーン
◆深さ／100
◆方向／上へ　◆シャドウモード／乗算
◆サイズ／5pixel　◆不透明度／75
◆方角／120
◆*Style/Inner Bevel*
◆*Technique/Smooth*
◆*Depth/100*
◆*Direction/Up*
◆*Size/5 pixels*
◆*Angle/120*
◆*Altitude/30*
◆*Highlight Mode/Screen*
◆*Shadow Mode/Multiply*
◆*Opacity/75*

⓬描画モードを「オーバーレイ」に設定
Set the blending mode to Overlay.

⓭「新規レイヤー作成」をクリック
Click Create a New Layer.

⓮グレースケールノイズにチェック
Check the Monochromatic box.

⓯水晶
Crystallize

⓰ぼかし（ガウス）
Blur (Gaussian)

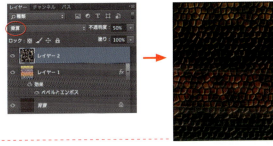

⓱描画モードを「乗算」に設定して完成
Set the blending mode to Multiply to finish the texture.

2) 色を変える　Changing the color

❶「レイヤー→画像の統合」でレイヤーを結合します。
1. In the Layer menu, choose Flatten Image to merge the layers.

❷メニューバー「イメージ」→「色調補正→色相・彩度」を選択します。
2. In the Image menu, choose Adjustments > Hue/Saturation.

❸プレビューで確認しながら「色相・彩度」のスライダーを動かしてイメージに近づけます。
3. Move the sliders of Hue/Saturation to try different values until the preview window shows the desired result.

※「色相」は色あいを、「彩度」は鮮やかさを、「明度」は明るさ暗さを調整します。
You can set each value to adjust the properties below:
Hue: Tones
Saturation: Vividness
Brightness: brightness and darkness

❶「色相・彩度」のスライダーで調整
Adjust the image with the sliders of Hue/Saturation.

「彩度」を左に−100で無彩色に
-100 saturation creates a grayscale texture.

「色相」を動かして別色に
Move the Hue slider to create color variations.

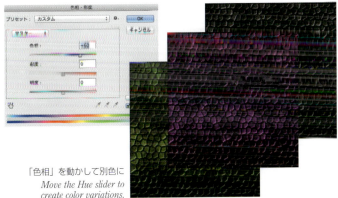

157

■ Do Photoshop

フィルターと「カスタムシェイプ」で作るラバープリント
Creating A Rubber Print Texture Using Filters and Custom Shape

1) ラバープリント　Rubber print

❶メニューバー「ファイル」から「新規」を選択し新規書類を作成します。
　◆「ファイル名」をダブルクリックし、名前を記入します。
　◆書類のサイズ／幅10cm×高さ10cm
　◆解像度／150pixel/inch
　◆カラーモード／RGBカラー
　◆カンバスカラー／白

1. In the File menu, choose New to create a new document.
　◆*Double-click the Name to enter a file name.*
　◆*Document Size/10cm in width and 10cm in height*
　◆*Resolution/150 Pixels/Inch*
　◆*Color Mode/RGB color*
　◆*Background Contents/White*

❷描画色を選びます。
2. Select a new foreground color.

❸メニューバー「フィルター→描画→雲模様1」を選択します。
3. In the Filter menu, choose Render > Clouds 1.

❹「テキストツール」で文字を入力します。
　◆フォント／Cooper Std : Black
4. Enter text with the Type tool.
　◆*Font style/Cooper Std: Black*

❺メニューバー「編集→変形→拡大・縮小」でイメージのサイズに拡大します。
5. In the Edit menu, choose Transform > Scale to enlarge the text to the desired size.

❻レイヤーパネル「スタイル」右上ボタンをクリックし、新規スタイルの中から「ボタン」を選択します。
6. In the Styles panel, click the button at the top-right corner and select Buttons in the new style menu.

❼ダイヤログの「OK」又は「追加」をクリックします。
7. Click OK or Append in the dialog box.

❽新規スタイル「ボタン」に置き換えられた中から「クリアエンボス」のアイコンをクリックします。
8. Click the Clear Emboss icon from the Buttons icons newly added in the Styles panel.

❾スタイルのアイコンをクリックで「レイヤースタイル」が適用されます。
9. The clicked layer style is instantly applied.

❶
◆ファイル名記入
◆書類のサイズ／
　幅10cm×高さ10cm
◆解像度／150pixel/inch
◆カラーモード／RGBカラー
◆カンバスカラー／白

◆*Enter a file name.*
◆*Document Size/*
　10cm in width and 10cm in height
◆*Resolution/150 Pixels/Inch*
◆*Color Mode/RGB color*
◆*Background Contents/White*

❷「描画色」を選ぶ
Select a new foreground color.

❸雲模様1
Clouds 1

◆テキストツールのオプションバーで「フォント」を選択
Select font style in the Options bar of the Type tool.

❹テキストツールで文字を入力
Type text with the Type tool.

❺「拡大・縮小」で文字を拡大
Enlarge the text with Scale.

「スタイル」パネルの右上をクリック
Click the icon at the top right corner of the Styles panel.

❻「ボタン」を選択
Choose Buttons.

❼「OK」をクリック
Click OK.

❽「クリアエンボス」のアイコンをクリック
Click the icon of Clear Emboss.

アイコンをダブルクリックでスタイル名が表示
You can dubble-click an icon to check the name of the style.

注）クリックのみで適用されるので元に戻る時はヒストリーパネルで戻るかあらかじめテキストレイヤーをコピーして試す
The style is instantly applied with a single-click, so create copies of the text layer or use the Undo command with the history panel when you want to try multiple styles.

❾適用されたレイヤースタイルが表示
The applied layer style appears.

※レイヤースタイル「クリアエンボス」適用
The result of the Clear Emboss layer style

158

■フォトショップで描く

2) カスタムシェイプ Custom Shape

❶ツールパネル「カスタムシェイプツール」を選択します。
 1. In the Tools panel, choose the Custom Shape tool.

❷オプションバー「シェイプ」のアイコンまたは▼印をクリックすると様々な種類のカスタムシェイプが表示されます。
 2. You can display various types of custom shapes by clicking the Shape icon or the triangle in the Options bar.

❶カスタムシェイプツール
 Custom Shape tool

❷シェイプのアイコンをクリック
 Click the shape icon.

❸ダイアログ右上のボタンをクリックし「動物」のシェイプを選択します。
 3. Click the button at the top right corner of the dialog box to choose the Animals shapes.

❸ダイアログ右上のボタンをクリック
 Click the button at the top right corner of the dialog box.

❹動物のシェイプに置き換えて選択
 Append the Animals shapes and make the selection.

❹「動物」のシェイプに置き換えられた中から鳩のアイコンを選択します。
 4. Choose the dove icon from the animal shapes list newly added.

❺左上から右下にかけてドラッグすると自動的に「シェイプ1」レイヤーが作成されます。
 5. Drag from the top-left to the bottom-right. A "Shape 1" layer is automatically created.

❺ドラッグで自動的にシェイプ作成
 The shape is automatically created after dragging over the image.

❻「スタイルパネル→クリアエンボス」のアイコンをクリックして完成です。
 6. In the Styles panel, click the icon of Clear Emboss to complete the shape.

❻「クリアエンボス」のアイコンをクリックでラバーのぬめり感が完成
 Click the Clear Emboss icon to add smooth and rounded effect of rubbers.

❼「移動ツール」で動かしながら微調整します。
 7. Adjust the position with the Move tool.

※スタイルパネルの右下にあるボタンの左から
　◆スタイルを消去
　◆新規スタイルを作成
　◆スタイルを削除
 In the order from left to right, each button at the right-bottom of the Styles panel:
 ◆clears a style.
 ◆creates a new style.
 ◆deletes a style.

◆スタイルを消去
 Clear the style
◆新規スタイルを作成
 Create a new style
◆スタイルを削除
 Delete the style

◆他にもさまざまなシェイプがあり、パネル上で任意のスタイルのアイコンをクリックして試しましょう。クリックに応じて画面が変化するのがわかります。
 Try other various styles by clicking any style icon in the panel. The image changes dynamically as you click a style icon.

◆さまざまなシェイプ *Multiple shapes*

赤い星 *Red Star*　　ベベル（マウスオーバー） *Beveled Mouseover*　　ダブルリング光彩 *Glowing Double Ring*

■ Do Photoshop

フィルターと「グラデーションマップ」で作るレオパード
Creating a Leopard Texture with Filters and Gradient Map

1）レオパード　*Leopard texture*

❶メニューバー「ファイル」から「新規」を選択し新規書類を作成します。
　◆「ファイル名」をダブルクリックし、名前を記入します。
　◆書類のサイズ／幅10cm×高さ10cm
　◆解像度／150pixel/inch
　◆カラーモード／RGBカラー
　◆カンバスカラー／白

1. In the File menu, choose New to create a new document.
　◆Double-click the Name to enter a file name.
　◆Document Size/10cm in width and 10cm in height
　◆Resolution/150 Pixels/Inch
　◆Color Mode/RGB color
　◆Background Contents/White

❷描画色を初期設定カラーにします。
2. Select the default foreground and background colors.

❸メニューバー「フィルター」「フィルターギャラリー」から「テクスチャ→ステンドグラス」を選択します。
　◆セルの大きさ／40
　◆境界線の太さ／20
　◆明るさの強さ／0

3. In the Filter menu, choose Filter Gallery > Stained Glass.
　◆Cell Size/40
　◆Border Thickness/20
　◆Light Intensity/0

❹「フィルター」から「ピクセレート→水晶」を選択します。
　◆セルの大きさ／16

4. In the Filter menu, choose Pixelate > Crystallize.
　◆Cell Size/16

❺「レイヤーパネル」の「背景」レイヤーを右下の「新規レイヤー作成」へドラッグし、「背景のコピー」レイヤーの不透明度を50%に設定します。

5. Drag the background layer onto Create a New Layer in the Layers panel and set the opacity of the "Background copy" to 50%.

❻「フィルター」から「その他→明るさの最小値」を選択します。
　◆半径／9ピクセル

6. In the Filter menu, choose Others > Minimum.
　◆Radius: 9 pixels

❼再度「フィルター」から「ピクセレート→水晶」を選択します。
　◆セルの大きさ／16

7. In the Filter menu, choose again Pixelate > Crystallize
　◆Cell Size/16

❽「レイヤーパネル」の右上ボタンを押して「表示レイヤーを結合」を選択し、2つのレイヤーを結合させます。

8. Click the button at the top-right corner of the Layers panel and select Merge Visible to merge the two layers.

❾「フィルター」から「ぼかし→ぼかし（ガウス）」を選択します。
　◆半径／4pixel

9. In the Filter menu, choose Blur > Gaussian Blur.
　◆Radius: 4 pixels

❶
◆ファイル名記入
◆書類のサイズ／
　幅10cm×高さ10cm
◆解像度／150pixel/inch
◆カラーモード／RGBカラー
◆カンバスカラー／白

◆*Enter a file name.*
◆*Document Size/*
　10cm in width and 10cm in height
◆*Resolution/150 Pixels/Inch*
◆*Color Mode/RGB color*
◆*Background Contents/White*

❸「ステンドグラス」
Stained Glass

❷「初期設定カラーを設定」ボタン
Default colors icon

❹「水晶」
Crystallize

❺「背景」をドラッグし「背景のコピー」作成し不透明度を50%に設定
Drag the background to create a "Background copy" and set its opacity to 50%.

❻「明るさの最小値」
Minimum

❼再度「水晶」
Choose Crystallize again.

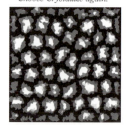

❽レイヤーパネルの右上ボタンを押し「表示レイヤーを結合」
Click the button at the top right corner of the Layers panel to select Merge Visible.

❾ぼかし（ガウス）
Gaussian Blur

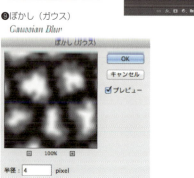

160

■フォトショップで描く

⓾メニューバー「イメージ→色調補正→グラデーションマップ」を選択し、「グラデーションマップ」部分をクリックして「グラデーションエディタ」を表示します。
10. In the Image menu, choose Adustments > Gradient Map and click the gradient to open the Gradient Editor.

⓫「開始点・分岐点・終了点」を順番にクリックし、カラーを表示、表示部分をクリックでカラーピッカーを表示します。
11. Set three color points in the order from the beginnnng point, changing point to the ending point by clicking above the gradient box, and click the gradient part to open the Color Picker.

⓬左から開始点、分岐点、終了点をダブルクリックし、「カラーピッカー」のカラーフィールドから、イメージの色をクリックしてカラー設定をします。
◆開始点／R/192、G/160、B/6
◆分岐点／R/48、G/15、B/2
◆終了点／R/209、G/160、B/2
12. Double-click the beginning point, changing point and ending point and click the desired color in the color field to set the gradient color.
◆*Beginning point/R/192, G/160, B/6*
◆*Changing point/R/48, G/15, B/2*
◆*Ending point/R/209, G/160, B/2*

⓭「新規グラデーション」をクリックで新規の設定カラーをプリセットに保存することができます。
13. You can click New to save the gradient as a preset.

⓮メニューバー「ファイル」から「新規→レイヤー」で「新規レイヤー」ダイアログで設定します。
◆描画モード／オーバーレイ
◆不透明度／100
◆オーバーレイの中性色で塗りつぶす（50%グレー）にチェックを入れます。
14. In the File menu, choose New > Layer and designate its setting in the New Layer dialog box.
◆*Blending mode/Overlay*
◆*Opacity/100*
◆*Check the box of Fill with Overlay-neutral color (50% gray).*

⓯グレーで塗りつぶされたレイヤーが作成されますが「オーバーレイモード」に設定されているので見た目の変化はありません。
15. A layer filled with gray is created, but its blending mode is Overlay. That is why the displayed image remains unchanged.

⓰フィルターから「ノイズ→ノイズを加える」を選択します。
◆量／120
◆「グレースケールノイズ」にチェック
16. In the Filter menu, choose Noise > Add Noise.
◆*Amount/120*
◆*Check the Monochromatic box.*

⓱ツールパネル「長方形選択ツール」で適当な部分を選択します。
17. Select the Rectangular Selection tool in the Tools panel and select any area on the image.

⓲フィルターから「変形→渦巻き」を選択します。
◆角度／190°
18. In the Filter menu, choose Transform > Twirl.
◆*Angle/190°*

⓳画像を見ながら「長方形選択ツール」を移動して「変形→渦巻き」を繰り返します。
19. Move the selection area and choose again Transform > Twirl, then repeat this process until the image shows the desired result.

※同じ場所で繰り返したり、部分的に少なくしたりランダムに適用することで、自然な毛足を感じさせることができます。
You can twirl several times one selection area and leave some areas totally unchanged to make unevenly twirled texture with natural-looking pile effect.

⓾グラデーション部分をクリックして「グラデーションエディタ」を表示
Click the gradient to open the Gradient Editor.

開始点、分岐点、終了点をクリック
Click the beginning point, changing point and ending point.

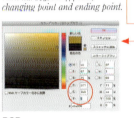

RGB
◆開始点／R/192、G/160、B/6
◆分岐点／R/48、G/15、B/2
◆終了点／R/209、G/160、B/2
RGB
◆*Beginning point/R/192, G/160, B/6*
◆*Changing point/R/48, G/15, B/2*
◆*Ending point/R/209, G/160, B/2*

⓭描画モードを「オーバーレイ」にして、「オーバーレイ中性色で塗りつぶす（50%グレー）」にチェックを入れます。
Set the blending mode to Overlay and check the box of Fill with Overlay-neutral color (50% gray).

⓯グレースケールノイズにチェック
Check the Monochromatic box.

⓱「変形→渦巻き」
Transform > Twirl

渦巻きをランダムに適用して自然な毛足を感じさせる
Create natural-looking effect by twirling unevenly the texture.

⓫「新規グラデーション」をクリックでプリセットに保存
Click New to save the gradient as a preset.

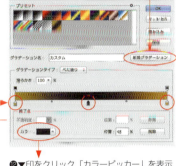

⓬▼印をクリック「カラーピッカー」を表示
Click the triangle to open the Color Picker.

「OK」クリックで描画
Click OK to apply the gradient.

⓮「オーバーレイモード」に設定されたレイヤー
Layer in the Overlay blending mode

⓰「長方形選択ツール」で部分的に選択
Choose the Rectangular Selection tool and select an area of the image.

161

■Do Photoshop

2) グラデーションマップ　*Gradient Map*

※グラデーションマップとは画像の明暗を、設定したグラデーションの色に置き換える機能です。
The Gradient Map changes the grayscale range of an image to the gradient colors newly designated.

❶「描画色」を選びメニューバー「色調補正→イメージ→グラデーションマップ」を選びます。
1. Select a new foreground color, then choose Adjustments > Gradient Map in the Image menu.

❷「グラデーションマップ→OK」で設定されます。
2. Click OK to apply the gradient map.

❸「グラデーションマップ」のグラデーション部分をクリックすると「グラデーションエディター」が表示されます。
3. You can click the gradient part of the Gradient Map to open the Gradient Editor.

❹「プリセット」の「黒、白」をクリックすると黒と白の色調で描画されます。
4. You can make the image black and white by clicking "Black, White" in the presets.

❺「プリセット」の「スペクトル」をクリックするとスペクトルの色調で描画されます。
5. You can paint the image in spectrum by clicking Spectrum in the presets.

❻「グラデーションエディター」ダイヤログボックスにはさまざまなプリセットが用意されており、プリセットの右上のボタンをクリックして読み込むことができます。
6. The Gradient Editor dialog box stores multiple presets, which you can load by clicking the button at the top right corner of the presets.

❼新規に読み込んだプリセット「ノイズサンプル」緑色系をクリックします。
7. Load a new preset named "Noise Sample" and click Green.

❽グラデーションエディター「カラーモデル」のスライダー「R/G/B」でカラー設定を変更することができます。
8. You can change the colors with the RGB sliders in the Color Model of the Gradient Editor.

❾「新規グラデーション」のボタンをクリックで変更した「新規の色調」をプリセットに登録することができます。
9. You can save the newly created color combination as a preset by clicking New in the dialog box.

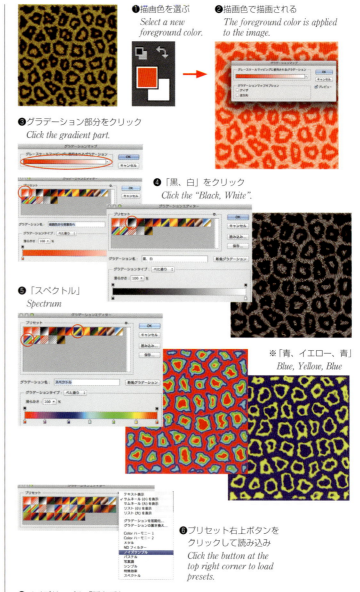

❶描画色を選ぶ *Select a new foreground color.*
❷描画色で描画される *The foreground color is applied to the image.*
❸グラデーション部分をクリック *Click the gradient part.*
❹「黒、白」をクリック *Click the "Black, White".*
❺「スペクトル」 *Spectrum*
※「青、イエロー、青」 *Blue, Yellow, Blue*

❻プリセット右上ボタンをクリックして読み込み *Click the button at the top right corner to load presets.*
❼ノイズサンプル「暖色系」 *Noise Sample "Warm colors"*
❽カラーモデルのスライダーで色の変更 *Change the color with the sliders in the Color Model.*
❾ボタンをクリックで色の登録 *Click the button to save the color settings.*

素材をデザイン画にマッピング
Adding Patterns and Textures to Clothing

「拡大・縮小」と「コピースタンプツール」で素材をマッピング
Adding a pattern to clothing with Scale and Clone Stamp

1) 素材をマッピングする　Adding a pattern to clothing

❶メニューバー「ファイル」から「開く」を選択「レオパードモデル1」とP159で完成させた「レオパード」を開きます。
1. In the File menu, choose File > Open to open the "Leopard Model 1" and "Leopard" completed in p.159.

❷ツールパネル「移動ツール」を選びます。
2. Choose the Move tool in the Tools panel.

❸「レオパード」をアクティブにして、「移動」ツールを「レオパード」の上でクリックしたまま移動したいファイル上にドラッグします。
3. Make the "Leopard" active and drag it onto the model image to which you apply the texture.

❹デザインに合わせてマッピングしやすいように「素材レイヤー」の不透明度を薄く設定（ここでは50％）しておきます。
4. Set the opacity of the texture in low level (50% is recommended here) to see the areas you should apply the texture through the top layer.

❺メニューバー「編集→拡大・縮小」を選択するとバウンディングボックスが表示されます。ボックス部分をドラッグして縮小します。
5. In the Edit menu, choose Scale to create a bounding box. Reduce the texture by dragging handles of the box.

❻「素材レイヤー」の不透明度を100％に戻します。
6. Reset the opacity of the texture to 100%.

❼ツールパネル「コピースタンプツール」を選びます。
7. Choose the Clone Stamp tool in the Tools panel.

❽画像の複製を開始する場所（コピー元）を、Altキー（Windows）／Optionキー（Macintosh）を押しながら、マウスでクリックします。
8. Alt-click (Windows) or option-click (Macintosh) an area you want to copy (an area you want to sample) on the texture.

❾複製したい場所でクリックしてコピーします。
9. Drag over the area of the model image where you want to apply the duplicaton to paint the texture.

※「調整あり」にチェックを入れるとペイント操作を中断して再開しても、複製した部分を続けてペイントすることができます。
　You can check the Aligned box to resume painting with the most current sampling point whenever you stop the painting.

❿ツールパネル「消しゴムツール」を選びます。毛足を感じさせるために、ブラシプリセットからブラシの先端を「はね」や「チョーク」のような先端を選びます。
10. Choose the Eraser tool in the Tools panel. Select a brush tip like Spatter or Chalk in the Brush Settings to create pile effect.

⓫外から内側に向かって消すと毛皮の毛立ち感が出やすくなります。
11. You can easily create raised nap effect of the fur by erasing in the inward direction.

❶開く
Open

❷移動させたオブジェクトは新規レイヤーになる
The moved object becomes a new layer.

❸移動ツール
Move tool

❹薄くする
Lower the opacity.

「リンク」をクリックで縦横の比率が同率
The aspect ratio can be locked by clicking the link icon.

「×」は破棄「○」は拡大・縮小の実行が適用
The scaling is canceled by the cross and applied by the circle.

❺バウンディングボックスをドラッグ
Drag handles of the bounding box.

❻不透明度を100％に戻す
Reset the opacity to 100%.

画像の同じ部分のコピーを複数の場所に適用する場合「調整あり」のチェックを外しておくとクリックの度、最初の複製ポイントから画像をペイントできます。
By unchecking the Alinged box, you can paint the sampled pixels from the initial sampling point each time you click to resume painting and can apply the same copy to multiple areas.

❼コピースタンプツールは指定した場所の画像をコピーして、別の場所にペイントする機能です。
The Clone Stamp tool samples pixels of a designated area and paint it over another area.

❽コピー元をクリック
Click the image you should sample.

❾複製したいところをクリックしてコピー
Click areas you want to paint the sampled pixels.

❿消しゴムツール
The Eraser tool

※薄くして消す部分を確認
Lower the opacity to see areas you need to erase.

⓫毛皮のタッチが出るようにランダムなブラシの先端を選ぶ
Choose rough brush tips to create fur effect.

■フォトショップで描く

衿の部分は大きく
Enlarge the texture for the collar part.

⓬身頃と同じく「移動ツール」でドラッグした
　レオパードを「拡大・縮小」で設定します。
12. As you did when you painted the bodice part, select the Move tool to drag the leopard texture and choose Scale to scale it.

⓭メニューバー「ファイル」から「開く」で
　「レオパードモデル」を開き、ドレスなど
　のレイヤーをドラッグして移動させます。
13. In the File menu, choose Open to open the "Leopard Model" to drag and move the dress layer and others.

⓮「グラデーションマップ」でドレスや小物
　の色に合わせて色を変更します。
14. Select a leopard color coordinating with the dress and accessories with the Gradient Map.

⓯ツールパネル「スポイトツール」を選択し
　ます。
15. In the Tools panel, choose the Eye Dropper tool.

⓰色を抽出したいところでクリックします。
16. Click color you want to sample in the image.

※スポイトツールはクリックした位置の色の
　情報を取得します。抽出した色は描画色に
　反映されます。
The Eye Dropper tool samples color data of a pixel you click. The foreground color box displays the sampled color.

⓱メニューバー「イメージ」「色調補正」「グラ
　デーションマップ」を選択します。
18. In the Image menu, choose Adjustments > Gradient Map.

⓲「OK」ボタンをクリックでレオパードが
　「描画色」のグラデーションに置き換えら
　れて完成です。
18. Click the OK button to complete coloring the leopard texture with the foreground color gradient.

◆色をワンクリックで変更
Change the color with a single-click.

165

- Do Photoshop

「自動選択ツール」で選択「色相・彩度」で色を変える
Selecting and Changing a Color Using Magic Wand Tool and Hue/Saturation.

1)「自動選択ツール」で選択し「雲模様」で塗りつぶす
Selecting with Magic Wand tool and fill with Clouds.

❶メニューバー「ファイル」から「開く」を選択「雲模様モデル1」を開きます。
1. In the File menu, choose Open to open the "Cloud Model 1".

❷ツールパネル「自動選択ツール」を選びます。
2. In the Tools panel, choose the Magic Wand tool.

※クリックした箇所と色が近い領域が自動的に選択されます。オプションバーでは許容値や隣接する領域かどうかの指定を行うことができます。
This tool automatically selects an area with a color similar to the pixel you click. You can designate the tolerance and decide whether the tool selects only adjacent areas using the same colors.

❸「背景」レイヤーをアクティブにして、ドレス部分をクリックして選択します。
3. Make the Background layer active to click and select a dress area.

❹「オプションバー」のアイコンをクリックして連続でドレス部分をすべて選択します。
4. Click the second icon from the left in the Options bar and select the other dress areas to select all the dress areas.

※Shiftを押しながらクリックでも、選択されている範囲に新たな選択範囲を追加できます。
You can add a new selection area to areas you already selected by shift-clicking it.

❶開く
Open

❷自動選択ツール
Magic Wand tool

❸「背景レイヤー」をアクティブにし、選択したい部分でクリック
Make the Background layer active and click on an area you want to select.

❹「自動選択ツール」オプション *The Options bar of the Magic Wand tool*

◆左から「新規選択」「現在の選択範囲に追加して選択する」「現在の選択範囲から削除する」「現在の選択範囲との共通部分を選択する」
From the left to right: New/Add To/Subtract From/Intersect With

◆許容値：選択する色の近似許容範囲を指定する値を小さくすると選択される範囲が狭くなり、多くすると範囲が広くなる

◆アンチエイリアス：範囲選択する境界線を滑らかにしたい場合にチェック

◆隣接：チェックでクリックした位置に隣接した部分から同系色の範囲が選択され、チェックされない場合、画像全体から同系色の範囲が選択される

◆全レイヤーを対象：全てのレイヤーから近似色を選択するか、選択された作業レイヤーだけ選択するか、全レイヤー使用をチェックオン／オフで選択

◆*Tolerance: designates the color range of selected pixels.*
A low value selects an small area, and a high value selects a large area.
◆*Anti-aliased: creates a smoother-edged selection.*
◆*Contiguous: selects only areas using the same color and adjacent to the clicked part. Otherwise, all pixels in the entire image using the same colors are selected.*
◆*Sample All Layers: Selects colors using data from all the visible layers. Otherwise, the Magic Wand tool selects colors only from the layer you are editing.*

1) 雲模様でいっきに彩色
Filling with colored clouds at a stretch.

❶描画色を選択します。
1. Select a new foreground color.

❷レイヤーパネルの「新規レイヤーを作成」ボタンをクリックし「レイヤー1」を作成します。
2. Click the Create a New Layer button to create a "Layer 1".

❸メニューバー「フィルター」から「描画→雲模様」を選択します。
3. In the Filter menu, choose Render > Clouds.

❹いっきに描画色の雲模様でドレス部分が塗りつぶされます。
4. The dress area is filled at a stretch with foreground color clouds.

❺レイヤーの名前を変更します。
5. Change the layer name.

※名前を付けたいレイヤーの上でダブルクリックして名前を入力します。
Double click on the layer you want to give a new name and type it.

※レイヤーをドラッグしてレイヤーの順も簡単に変更することができます。
You can easily change order of the layers by dragging them.

❶「描画色」
The foreground color

❷「新規レイヤーを作成」
Create a New Layer

❸「雲模様」を選択
Choose Clouds.

❹「描画色」で塗りつぶされた雲模様
Foreground color clouds

3) 色相・彩度で色を変える
Changing a color with Hue/Saturation.

❶レイヤーパネルの「ピンク」を「新規レイヤーを作成」ボタンにドラッグし「ピンク」のコピーを作成します。
1. In the Layers panel, drag the "Pink" on the Create a New Layer button to make a copy of it.

❷レイヤー「ピンク」の「表示・非表示」のアイコンをクリックして非表示にし「ピンクのコピー」をアクティブにします。
2. Click the Show/Hide icon of the "Pink" layer to hide it and make the "Pink copy" active.

❶レイヤー「ピンク」を「新規レイヤー作成」ボタンにドラッグ
1. Drag the "Pink" on the Create a New Layer button.

❷「ピンク」を非表示にし「ピンクのコピー」をアクティブにする
2. Hide the "Pink" and make the "Pink copy" active.

❸メニューバー「イメージ」から「色調補正→色相・彩度」を選択し、「色相」のスライダーを動かし色を変更します。
3. In the Image menu, choose Adjustments > Hue/Saturation to move the hue slider and change the color.

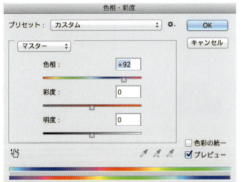

◆色相：色の属性の一つで、赤や青といった色味の違い
◆彩度：画像や映像などの鮮やかさの度合い
◆明度：色の属性のひとつで、その色の明暗の度合い
　（明度が100％であれば白に、0％であれば黒になる）

◆*Hue: is a color property referring to a color family.*
◆*Saturation: is degree of color intensity in an image or a picture.*
◆*Brightness: is a color property referring the lightness and darkness of a color.*
　(100% brightness make the color white and 0% make it black)

❹メニューバー「ファイル」から「開く」を選択「雲模様モデル2」を開きます。
4. In the File menu, choose Open to open the "Clouds Model 2".

❺「バッグ」や「アクセサリー」を選択しドラッグ＆ドロップで「雲模様モデル1」に加えて完成させる。
5. Select the "Bag" and "Accecories". Then drag, drop and add them to the "Clouds Model 1" to complete the design.

■ Do Photoshop

「パターンの定義」と「変形」でマッピング
Adding a Texture to Clothing with Define Pattern and Transform

1)保存したパターンで塗りつぶしてマッピング　Filling an area with a saved pattern and adding it to clothing

❶メニューバー「ファイル」から「開く」を選択「チェックモデル2」と「ギンガムチェック」を開きます。
1. In the File menu, choose Open to open the "Check Model 2" and "Gingham Check".

❷ツールパネル「長方形選択ツール」で柄の送りを考慮しながら選択します。
2. Select one repeat exactly with Rectangular Marquee tool in the Tools panel.

❸ファイル「編集→パターンを定義」でパターンとして登録します。
3. In the Edit menu, choose Define Pattern to save the selection area as a pattern.

❹レイヤーパネル「新規レイヤーを作成」ボタンをクリックして新規レイヤーを作成します。
4. In the Layers panel, click Create a New Layer to create a new layer.

❺「新規レイヤー」でツールパネル「長方形選択ツール」でドラッグして選択範囲を確定します。
5. Drag over the new layer with the Rectangular Marquee tool in the Tools panel to make a selection area.

❻ファイル「編集→塗りつぶし」を選び、操作ウインドウの中から「パターン」を選択します。
6. Choose Fill in the Edit menu, and choose Pattern in the dialog box.

❼「カスタムパターン」から先程、新規登録した「ギンガム」を選択します。
7. From the Custom Pattern, choose "Gingham" newly saved in the step 3.

❶「チェックモデル2」 "Check Mode 2"

❷「長方形選択ツール」でギンガムチェックを選択
Select one repeat of the gingham check pattern exactly with the Rectanglar Marquee tool

❸「パターンを定義」で新規パターンとして登録
Save the repeat as a new pattern with Define Pattern.

❹「新規レイヤーを作成」をクリックして「レイヤー2」を作成
Click Create a New Layer to create the "Layer 2".

❺大きめに選択する
Make a larger selection area.

❻「塗りつぶし→パターン」を選択
Choose Fill > Pattern.

❼「カスタムパターン」から新規登録されたギンガムを選択する
Select the gingham check pattern newly saved from the Custom Pattern.

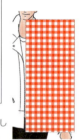

❽パターンで塗りつぶし
Fill with the pattern.

2)「変形→回転→ワープ」 Transform > Rotate > Warp

❶メニューバー「編集→変形→回転」を選択し、矢印で回転させます。
1. In the Edit menu, choose Transform > Rotate to rotate the pattern with an arrow cursor.

❷次に「変形・ワープ」を選択すると、ハンドルとは少し異なるメッシュが表示されます。
2. Choose Transform > Warp to display a mesh, which is a little different from the handle.

❸方向線の端の点を操作して、変形部分のカーブの度合いを、服に合わせて調整します。
3. In accordance with the cloth shape, adjust curves of the texture by moving control points of the mesh.

❹ツールパネル「自動選択ツール」を選び「背景レイヤー」で選択したい部分をクリックします。
4. In the Tools panel, choose Magic Wand tool to click the part you want to select in the background layer.

❺「ギンガムチェック」レイヤーを選びメニューバー「選択範囲・選択範囲の反転」を選びます。
5. Select the "Gingham check" and choose Reverse in the Selection menu.

❶変形→回転
Transform > Rotate

❷変形→ワープ
Transform > Warp

❸「○」で確定
Click the circle to complete the transformation.

❹「背景」をアクティブにする
Make the "Background" active.

❺「自動選択ツール」でジャケット部分を選択し、反転させる
Select the jacket area with the Magic Wand tool and reverse the selecton area.

168

■フォトショップで描く

3)「選択の反転」でデリート Selecting Reverse and deleting the selection area.

❶「delete」キーを押すと選択範囲が消去されます。
1. Press the delete key to delete the selection area.

❷他の部分もパターンで塗りつぶし、変形、反転、deleteで仕上げます。
2. Complete the other areas by filing with the texture, transforming, rotating, and deleting.

❸「背景」に戻り「自動選択ツール」で袖や衿部分を選択しブラシで仕上げます。
3. Return to the "Background", and select the sleeve and collar parts with the Magic Wand tool. Complete them with brushes.

❸「ブラシ」のオプション「流量」を30%くらいに設定すると柔らかく仕上がる
Setting the Flow to about 30% in the brush option enables you to create soft effect on the areas.

❹「レイヤー1」を「新規レイヤー作成」にドラッグしてコピーを作成します。
4. Create a "Layer 1 copy" and hide the "Layer 1".

❹「レイヤー1」のコピーを作成し「レイヤー1」は非表示にする
Drag the "Layer 1" on Create a New Layer to copy it.

❺メニューバー「イメージ→色調補正→色相・彩度」でパンツの色を変更します。
5. In the Image menu, choose Adjustments > Hue/Saturation to change the pants color.

※黒や白など色味のない無彩色を変更する時は「色彩の統一」にチェックを入れます。
The Colorize box should be checked to colorize a grayscale image.

169

Do Photoshop

スキャン画像を「レベル補正」で調整
Adjusting a Scanned Image with Levels

1)「レベル補正」で線を強調しデザインを補正する
Adjusting a design by highlighting lines with Levels

❶メニューバー「ファイル」から「開く」を選択「レベル補正モデル下絵」を開きます。
1. In the File menu, choose Open to open the "Levels Model Sketch".

❷「色調補正→レベル補正」のアイコンをクリックして「レベル補正パネル」を表示します。
2. Click the Adjustments icon > Levels icon to open the Levels panel.

❸画面のプレビューを確認しながら「ハイライト」を左に「シャドー」を右にスライダーを移動します。
3. Move the Highlight slider to left and the Shadow slider to the right until the preview window shows the disired result.

❹レイヤーパネルの右上のアイコンをクリックして「画像を統合」または「下のレイヤーと統合」を選んで「レベル補正1」を「背景」に統合します。
4. Click the icon at the right side of the top in the Layers panel to select Flatten Image or Merge Down and merge the "Levels Model Sketch" to the "Background".

※部分的に修正したい時には、別に描いた修正部分を貼付けて補正が簡単にできます。ここではスカートのシルエットを補正します。
When you want to modify an area of the design, you can draw the modified area separately and paste it to the design. In this section, you modify only the skirt area.

❺「背景」を「新規レイヤーを作成」ボタンにドラッグして「背景のコピー」を作製します。
5. Drag the "Background" on the Create a New Layer button to create "Background copy".

❻「背景のコピー」の「塗り」の％を落して「なげなわツール」でスカート部分を囲みます。
6. Lower the fill percentage of "Background copy" and surround the skirt area with the Lasso tool.

❼「移動ツール」で囲ったスカートを移動します。
7. Move the surrounded skirt area with the Move tool.

❽「消しゴムツール」で「背景」の修正したいスカート部分を消します。
8. Erase the skirt area you want to modify on "Background" with the Eraser tool.

❾「背景のコピー」の「塗り」を100％に戻し「モード」を乗算にして統合します。
9. Reset the Fill value of "Background copy" to 100% and set the blending mode to multiply. Then, merge them.

❿「背景のコピー」を作製しモードを「乗算」にします。「背景」の表示は非表示にします。
10. Create "Backgound copy"and set its mode to multiply. Hide "Background".

⓫「背景のコピー」の下に「新規レイヤー」を作製、クリックして名前を付けます。
11. Create a new layer below the "Background copy" and click it to name a name.

⓬「背景のコピー」をアクティブにし「自動選択ツール」で肌の部分をクリックして選択します。
12. Make "Background copy" active, then click and select the skin area with Magic Wand tool.

⓭肌レイヤーをアクティブにします。
13. Make the skin layer active.

❶「レベル補正モデル下絵」
"Levels Model Sketch"

❷アイコンをクリック
Click the icon

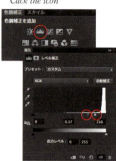

❸ハイライトのスライダーを左に、シャドースライダーを右に移動して画面を明るく線を強調する
Lighten the entire image and highlight the outline of the sketch by moving the highlight slider to left and the shadow slider to right.

❹レベル補正を背景に統合
Merge "Levels Model Sketch" to "Background"

❺背景をドラッグしてコピー
Drag "background" to copy it

※クリック

❻塗りの％を落してなげなわツールで囲む
Lower the fill percentage and surround with the Lasso tool.

❼「移動ツール」で囲ったスカートを移動
Move the surrounded skirt with the Move tool.

❽消しゴムツールで背景のスカートを消す
Erase the background skirt with the Eraser tool.

❾「塗り」を100％に戻しモードを「乗算」にして統合する
Reset the Fill to 100% and set the blending mode to Multiply to merge them.

❿背景のコピーを作製しモードを乗算にする
Create "Background copy" and set its blending mode to Multiply.

⓫背景のコピーの下に新規レイヤーを作製
Create a new layer below "Background copy"

⓬「背景のコピー」をアクティブにし「自動選択ツール」で肌の部分を選択する
Make "Background copy" active, then click and select the skin part with the Magic Wand tool.

⓭肌レイヤーをアクティブにする
Make the skin layer active

2) 選択は「背景のコピー」で塗りは「レイヤー」で
Selecting areas on the "Background copy" and paint each layers

❶「ブラシツール」のオプションからブラシの先端アイコンをクリックし「ソフト円ブラシ」を選択します。
1. Click the brush tip icon in the Options bar of the Brush tool and select the Soft Circle Brush.

❷「描画色」と「背景色」に肌色の濃淡を入れ、入れ替えつつ「流量」を30%程に調整し、ぼかし塗ります。
2. Change the foreground and background color to two different skin tones, set the Flow to about 30% and paint the skin areas by using the two different colors alternately.

❶「ソフト円ブラシ」を選択
Select Soft Circle Brush

❷「描画色」
Foreground color

❸「背景のコピー」の下に「新規レイヤー」を作製し、髪やドレス、バッグの色を各レイヤーに分けて塗ります。
3. Create new layers separately for the hair, dress and bag area below the "Background copy", and paint them.

❹バッグに色を塗りメニューバー「フィルター→エンボス」を選び角度と高さを調整します。
4. Paint the bag and choose Emboss in the Filter menu, then adjust its angle and height.

❺サングラスの「レイヤー」は「背景のコピー」の上にします。
5. Move the "Sunglasses" layer above the "Background copy".

171

Do Photoshop

「ブラシプリセット」でプリント柄
Creating a Print Texture with Brush Settings

「ブラシプリセット」は、サイズ、シェイプ、硬さなどの特性が定義されたブラシ先端です。「ブラシ先端のシェイプ」タブでは、ブラシのサイズや硬さ、傾きの角度、立体感をだす真円率、間隔を設定できます。ブラシの設定をカスタマイズして、ライブラリに追加することも可能です。

Brush Settings stores brush tips defined with their size, shape and hardness. In the Brush Tip Shape menu, you can select brush size, hardness, angle, roundness (which helps you to add three-dimentional effect), and spacing. You can also create a new brush setting and add it to the brush library.

1)「ブラシプリセット」 *Brush Settings*

❶ アイコンをクリックで「ブラシプリセット」が表示されます。
1. Click the icon to open Brush Settings

❷ アイコンをクリックで「ブラシの先端シェイプ」が表示されます。
2. Click the icon to open "Brush Tip Shape".

❸ マスター「直径」でブラシサイズを一時的に変更します。スライダーをドラッグか、値を入力します。
3. Change the brush size by moving the slider or entering a value of Size.

❹「ブラシ先端のシェイプ」の「間隔」にチェックを入れて重ならないようにスライダーをドラッグするか、値を入力します。
4. Check the Spacing?box of the Brush Settings Panel and drag the slider or enter a new value to maintain the distance between the brush marks.

※ブラシのサンプルで特定の形になっているものを選び、間隔を調整すると、ブレードやレースなどの縁飾りを簡単に描くことができます。
 You can draw easily edge decoration like braids and lace by selecting a specific brush tip and adjust the Spacing.

❺「ブラシプリセットパネル」の右上▼ボタンをクリックし、ブラシファイルの読み込みで追加します。
5. Click the triangle in the top right corner of the?Brush Settings panel to load and add a brush file.

❻ 表示ダイアログで「OK」をクリックして現在のリストを置き換えるか、「追加」ボタンをクリックして現在のリストに追加します。
6. Click OK in the opened dialog box to replace the current list with the loaded brush file, or click Append to append it to the current list.

❶ アイコンをクリックして「ブラシプリセット」を表示
Click the icon to open the Brush Settings

❷「ブラシ先端のシェイプ」を表示
Open the Brush Tip Shape

❸ マスター「直径」の値をスライダーをドラッグでサイズを変更
Change the size by entering a value to Size or dragging the slider

❹「間隔」にチェックを入れ値かスライダーをドラッグして間隔を自由に変更
Check Spacing, then set the value or drag the slider to change freely the spacing.

❺ 新規ブラシの読み込み
Load a new brush

❻「追加」で新規ブラシを加える
Click Add to add the new brush

2) ブラシの機能拡張の追加 *Adding brush extension*

❶ ブラシパネルには、変化する要素を追加してブラシ先端をプリセットするためのさまざまなオプションが用意されています。
1. The Brush panel provides many options, which you can change to add random effect to brush strokes and save it as a new brush preset.

❷「シェイプ」にチェックを入れコントロールの「フェード」の値を入れて描くと自然にフェードアウトします。他にも「散布」や「カラー」など、さまざまなブラシ機能を試してみましょう。
2. You can draw fading strokes by checking Shape?Dynamics, setting the Control to Fade and entering a value. Try other various brush functions like "Scatter" or "Color Dynamics".

❶「ブラシ先端のシェイプ」のオプション
Option of Brush Tip Shape

❷「フェード」
Fade

2)「フェード」でパネル柄 *Creating panel patterns with Fade*

❶ メニューバー「ファイル」から「開く」を選択し「ブラシモデル1」を開きます。
1. In the File menu, choose Open to open "Brush Model 1"

❷「シェイプ→コントロール：フェード」の値を設定、「カラー」に「描点ごとに適用」にチェックを入れ「色相のジッター」の順に設定します。
2. Choose Shape Dynamics > Control > Fade and enter a value in the box. Then choose the Color Dynamics, check the Apply Per Tip and set the value of Hue Jitter.

❷「シェイプ・散布・カラー」
  Shape Dynamics, Scattering, Color Dynamics

❸「自動選択ツール」で「背景」のキャミソール部分を選択し「レイヤー1」で描画します。
3. Select the camisole part on Background with the Magic Wand tool and apply the print on "Layer 1".

❹ 下から上に向かって描くとフェード効果でパネル柄のように表現できます。
4. You can paint a natural panel pattern with fade effect by drawing upward.

❶ 開く
  Open

■ Do Photoshop

「ペンタブレット」で描く
Using a Pen Tablet

　靴やバッグ等の硬質なものや平面図のようなデザイン画を描く時に「ペンタブレット」を使用することで、自由でいながらも確かな線で描くことができます。

Using a pen tablet allows us to draw a fashion illustration of shoes, bags and other firm items or a technical drawing with smooth and balanced lines.

1) 写真を下地にデザイン線を描く　*Tracing the outline of an item in a photo*

❶ メニューバー「ファイル」から「新規」を選択し、プリセットからサイズ「A4」を解像度150で作成します。

1. In the File menu, choose New to select A4 from the presets menu and set the resolution to 150.

❷ ファイルから「埋め込みを配置」で「ハイヒール」を配置し、「レイヤー」の不透明度を薄くします。

2. In the File menu, choose Place Embedded to place the "High Heel" and lower its opacity.

❸ 「新規レイヤー」を作成し名前を「線画」にします。

3. Create a new layer and name it "Outline".

❹ 「ブラシ」のオプションバーから「ブラシプリセット」を開きます。「シェイプ」の「コントロール」を「筆圧」に設定し、「ブラシの先端シェイプ」でサイズを選びます。

4. Select the Brush tool to open the Brush Settings from the Options bar, then set the Control of the Shape to Pen Pressure and select the size in the Brush Tip Shape.

❶ 新規書類を作成
　◆「ファイル名」を記入
　◆ 書類のサイズ／A4
　　（210mm×297mm）
　◆ 解像度／150pixel/inch
　◆ カラーモード／RGBカラー
　◆ カンバスカラー／白

Create a new document.
◆Enter a file name
◆Document Size/A4
*　(210 mm in width and*
*　297 mm in height)*
◆Resolution/150pixels/Inch
◆Color Mode/RGB Color
◆Background Content/White

※「ブラシプリセット」
のアイコン
Brush Settings icon

❷「埋め込みを配置」したレイヤーの不透明度を薄く設定する

Lower the opacity of the layer placed with Place Embedded.

❸「新規レイヤー」を作成し、名前を付ける

Create a new layer and name it

※「ブラシの先端シェイプ」で「直径」のサイズを選ぶ
Designate the Size in the Brush Tip Shape

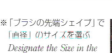

❹「シェイプ」のコントロールを「筆圧」に設定します

Set the Control of the Shape to Pen Pressure.

※「筆圧」を設定するとプレビューで強弱のついた線が示されます

Selecting Pen Pressure displays an uneven line in the brush stroke preview.

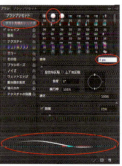

■フォトショップで描く

2) ペンタブレットで線を描く
Drawing a line using a pen tablet

❶「レイヤー線画」に紙に描くのと同じ要領で下絵の写真に沿って線を描きます。
1. Place a point on the outline in the black smooth to draw a line on the "Outline" layer in the manner of drawing a sketch on a tracing paper.

※写真に忠実に描こうとすると、かえって歪んだ線になってしまいます。下絵から離れてもかまわず、勢いよく描くのがツボ。
Trying to trace exactly the outline of the photo rather results in drawing a rough outline. The point is to draw confidently without concern for drawing a swerving outline.

❷メニューバー「編集→変形→ワープ」を選ぶとメッシュ状のバウンディングボックスが表示されます。下絵に沿うようにコントロールポイントやメッシュ内の領域を動かします。
2. In the Edit menu, choose Transform > Warp to display a mesh bounding box. Move control points and sections of the mesh to transform the line along the photo.

❸「新規レイヤー」を「線画」の上に作成します。
3. Create a new layer above the "Outline".

❹「新規レイヤー」に次の線を描きます。
4. Trace the next part of the outline.

❺「ワープ」で線を下絵に沿わせて確定し、余分な線は消しゴムで消します。
5. Transform the line along the photo with Warp, then erase unnecessary parts with the Eraser tool.

❻「新規レイヤー」に描かれた線が確定したら必ず、線画のレイヤーに結合します。
6. When you determine a line on the new layer, make sure of merging it to the "Outline" layer.

❼新たに「新規レイヤー」を作成し、次の線を描き、同じ手法を繰り返しボディの部分を完成させます。
7. Create a new layer and trace the next part of the outline. Repeat the same process to complete drawing the shoe bodice outline.

❽「線画」の下に「新規レイヤー」を作成し、白で塗りつぶします。また、必ず「線画」に統合します。
8. Create a new layer below the "Outline" and fill it with white. Make sure of merging it to the "Outline".

❾「自動選択ツール」でボディ以外の部分を選択し「delete」で削除します。
9. Select the entire area except for the shoe bodice with the Magic Wand tool and press the Delete key to delete the selection area.

※ヒール部分は別レイヤーを作成し同じ手法で完成します。
Similarly, create other layers for the heel part to draw and complete it.

❶力を入れると太く、力を抜けば細い線に。取り消しのショートカットキーを使って何度も思い通りの線になるまで描くのがコツ
Pen pressure dynamically changes width of the strokes. The point is to try drawing as many lines as possible for the desired result by using the Undo shortcut.

❷「ワープ」で表示されるメッシュ状の領域内やコントロールポイントを動かして微妙な曲線を調整
Adjust lines to create delicate curves by moving control points and sections of the mesh displayed after choosing Warp.

❸「線画」の上に「新規レイヤー」を作成
Create a new layer above the "Outline".

❹「新規レイヤー」の上に必ず次の線を描く
Make sure of drawing the next part of the outline on the new layer.

❺「ワープ」で線を調整
Adjust lines with Warp.

❻「レイヤー1」で描かれた線は必ず「線画」に統合
Make sure of merging the line of the "Layer 1" to the "Outline".

※下絵から外れていても勢いよく描くことがコツ
The point is to draw confidently without concern of swerving line.

※同じ手法を繰り返しながらボディの部分を完成させる
Repeat the same process to complete the shoe bodice outline.

❼次の線を描く時は必ず「新規レイヤー」を作成して描く
Make sure of creating a new layer to draw the next line.

※「背景」を非表示にすると透明に描かれているのがよく分かる
You can check that the outline is made on the transparent layer by hiding the "Background".

❽「線画」の下に「新規レイヤー」を作成
Create a new layer below the "Outline"

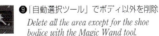

❾「自動選択ツール」でボディ以外を削除
Delete all the area except for the shoe bodice with the Magic Wand tool.

※ボディとヒールを別のレイヤーにしてヒールのバリエーション作成
Separating the bodice layer and heel layer allows us to make easily heel variations.

3）ブラシで描画
Drawing with a brush

❶「レイヤー線画」をアクティブにし、「自動選択ツール」で着色部分を選択します。
1. Make the "Outline" active and select the area to be colored with the Magic Wand tool.

❷「新規レイヤー」を作成し「ブラシ」の直径をソフト円ブラシに、流量を30％に設定して描画します。
2. Create a new layer and set the brush tip to a soft circle brush and the Flow to about 30%, then paint the area.

❸「レイヤー2」にボディ部分を着色します。
3. Create a "Layer 2" to paint the bodice part.

❹レイヤー「ヒール1」を表示し「自動選択ツール」で選択し「新規レイヤー」に描画します。
4. Show the "Heel 1" to select the heel part with the Magic Wand tool, and paint it with a new layer.

※バリエーションを作る時は各々のレイヤーに名前を付けて分かりやすくします。
Aa

❺「レイヤー2」のコピーを作成し「レイヤースタイル→グラディーションオーバーレイ」の黒から白を設定します。
5. Create a copy of the "Layer 2" and choose Layer Styles > Gradient Overlay to apply the "Black to White".

❻「ヒール2」の着色レイヤーを「ヒール2-a」と名前を付けて、ボディと同じ手順で仕上げます。
6. Create a new layer named "Heel 2-a" to paint the Heel 2 area, and complete the new layer in the same process.

❼最初に配置した写真の「ハイヒール」レイヤーのコピーを作成し「ヒール1-a」の上に移動します。「装飾」と名付けます。
7. Create a copy of the high-heel photo layer placed in the beginning and move the copy below the "Heel 1-a", then change its name to "Ornament".

❽写真の装飾以外の部分を「自動選択ツール」や「消しゴムツール」で消去します。
8. Delete and erase all the areas except for the ornament on the copy with the Magic Wand tool and the Eraser tool.

※「消しゴムツール」のペンタブレットの筆圧で細かい部分も簡単に消すことができます。
You can easily erase small areas by using a pen tablet with the Pen Pressure mode of the Eraser tool.

❾「ワープ」で「ヒール1」に合わせてサイズを合わせ「トーンカーブ」や「レベル補正」で調整して仕上げます。
9. Transform the ornament along the "Heel 1" with Warp, then adjust and complete it with Curves and Levels.

❶「自動選択ツール」で底部分を選択
Select the sole part with the Magic Wand tool.

❷「レイヤー1」で描画する
Paint on the "Layer 1".

※流量を30％位に設定すると柔らかい濃淡のある塗りができる
Setting the Flow to about 30% allows you to apply a soft gradient.

❸「レイヤー2」にボディ部分を描画
Paint the bodice part on the "Layer 2".

注）選択は必ず「線画」のレイヤーで！描画する時は「レイヤー1」で！
Note: Make sure of selecting the area on the "Outline" layer and painting it on the "Layer 1".

❹「ヒール1」で選択しレイヤー「ヒール1-a」で描画する
Select the area on the "Heel 1" and paint it on the "Heel 1-a".

※ヒールのレイヤーが必ずボディ線画の上にくるように順番に注意
Make sure of positioning the heel layer above the bodice layers.

❺「レイヤー2」のコピーを作成
Create a copy of the "Layer 2".

❻「ヒール2-a」も同じレイヤー効果
Add the same layer effect to the "Heel 2-a".

※グラデーションのバランスをスライダーで調整する
Adjust the changing point of the gradient with the slider.

❼「ハイヒール」のコピーを作成し「ヒール2-a」の上に移動
Create a copy of the photo layer and position it above the "Heel 2-a".

❽「消しゴムツール」で装飾以外を消す
Erase all the areas except for the ornament part with the Eraser tool.

※「トーンカーブ」や「レベル補正」で調整
Adjust it with Curves and Levels.

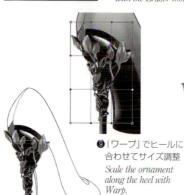

❾「ワープ」でヒールに合わせてサイズ調整
Scale the ornament along the heel with Warp.

4) Tシャツを描く
Drawing a T-shirt

■メニューバー「ファイル」から「埋め込みを配置」で「Tシャツ」を配置します。
1. In the File menu, choose Place Embedded to place the T-shirt.

■「ブラシ」のオプションバーから「ブラシプリセット」を開きます。「シェイプ」の「コントロール」を「筆圧」に設定し「ブラシの先端シェイプ」でサイズを選びます。
2. In the brush option bar, open the Brush Settings to set the Control of the Shape to Pen Pressure and select the size in the Brush Tip Shape menu.

■「新規レイヤー」に丸首の部分を描き「ワープ」で曲線を調整します。
3. Draw a front neckline on a new layer and adjust its curve with Warp.

■「新規レイヤー」に丸首の後ろ部分を描き「ワープ」で調整した後、必ずレイヤーを統合します。
4. Draw a back neckline on another new layer and adjust it with Warp, then be sure to merge the two new layers.

■肩のラインの直線は「shift」を押しながら引くと「垂直又は水平」の線を描くことができます。
5. You can easily draw the shoulder line by drawing straight lines while holding down the Shift key to draw a vertical or horizontal line.

※「shift」を押し続けて描くと、次に引く線に45度の角度で連続した線になるので、必ず一度「shift」を離してから次の線を描きます。
Make sure of releasing the Shift key before drawing the next line. Otherwise, the next line will be a continuous line forming an angle of 45° with respect to the previous line.

■「編集→自由変形」で肩のラインに沿わせます。直線部分の脇や裾の部分を描く時も「新規レイヤー」で描き、一枚のレイヤーに統合して完成させます。
6. In the Edit menu, choose Free Transform to adjust the lines along the shoulder lines of the photo. Make sure of creating a new layer to draw a new line and merge it to the other layer when you draw any side or hem lines.

※この時点で「Tシャツと背景」レイヤーを非表示にすると透明セルに描かれた線画のみ表示されます。
At this step, hiding the "T-shirt" and "Background" layers shows the outline drawn on the transparent background.

■統合したレイヤーの下に「新規レイヤー」を作成し白で塗りつぶした後、必ず「線画」に統合します。
7. Create a new layer below the "Outline" and fill the new layer with white. Be sure to merge it to the "Outline".

■Tシャツ以外の背景を「自動選択ツール」で選択し「delete」で消去して選択を解除します。
8. Select the entire area except for the T-shirt part with the Magic Wand tool and press the Delete key to delete it. Then, deselect the area.

■「自動選択ツール」で着色する部分を選択し「描画色と背景色」の色を設定した後、「新規レイヤー」を作成し、フィルターから「描画→雲模様1」を選択で描画します。
9. Select the areas to be painted with the Magic Wand tool, then select a new foreground and background color. Create a new layer and choose Render > Clouds 1 to paint the areas.

❶「埋め込みを配置」でTシャツを配置する
Place the T-shirt image with Place Embedded.

❷「ブラシ」の筆圧で線を調整
Draw a delicate neckline with the Pen Pressure mode of the Brush tool.

❸「ワープ」で丸首を調整
Adjust the front neckline with Warp.

❹丸首の後ろ部分も調整
Adjust the back neckline too.

❺直線は「shift」を押しながら描く
Adjust lines with Warp.5. Draw straight lines while holding down the Shift key.

※「長方形選択ツール」で大きく選択
Make a big selection area on the line with the Rectangular Selection tool

❻「編集→自由変形」で角度を合わせる
Adjust angle with Free Transform in the Edit menu.

❼「線画」の下に「新規レイヤー」を白で塗りつぶし「線画」に統合
Create a new layer filled with white below the "Outline" and merge them.

※Tシャツと背景レイヤーを非表示
Hide the "T-shirt" and "Background" layers.

❽「自動選択ツール」でTシャツ以外の部分を選択し「delete」で消去
Select the entire area except for the T-shirt part with the Magic Wand tool and delete the area by pressing the Delete key.

❾Tシャツの描画部分を選択し「描画→雲模様1」で塗りつぶす
Select the areas to be painted of the T-shirt and fill them by choosing Clouds 1 in the Render menu.

※選択した描画色と背景色で描画される
Clouds are painted with the selected foreground and background colors.

■Do Photoshop

「レイヤーマスク」でマスキングする
Masking out Part of an Image with a Layer Mask

「レイヤーマスク」は、レイヤーの画像を消去せず、一時的にレイヤーの一部を透明や半透明にできる特殊なマスクです。大きなプリント柄などの位置を決めるときに、不要な部分をマスクしてプリント柄の位置を変えたり、グラデーションで消すことができます。実際に画像を切り抜いている訳ではないので何度でもやり直しが可能で、デザインの変更が簡単にできます。

Layer masks are special masks allowing you to make a part of a layer temporarily transparent or translucent without deleting the layer. You can mask an unnecessary area of a print texture to easily change its position or create fading effect. The original image remains uncut, so you can redo any number of times and easily change a design.

1) レイヤーマスクで柄位置を自由に変更 *Changing pattern position freely with layer masks.*

❶メニューバー「ファイル」から「開く」を選択「レイヤーマスクモデル1」と「プリント」を開きます。
1. In the File menu, choose Open to open "Layer Mask Model 1" and "Print".

❷「移動ツール」で「プリント」を「レイヤーマスクモデル1」にドラッグして移動します。
2. Drag and move "Print" on "Layer Mask Model 1" with the Move tool.

❸移動した「レイヤー1」の「不透明度」の数値を下げて薄くするか、モードを「乗算」にして、「背景」のデザイン線が見えるようにします。
3. Set a lower value to the opacity?of the moved "Layer 1" to make it translucent, or set the Blending mode to Multiply to see the design of the Background layer.

❹「背景レイヤー」をアクティブにします。
4. Make the Background layer active.

❺「自動選択ツール」で、プリントを表示させたい部分をクリックして選択範囲を作成します。
5. With the?Magic Wand tool, click the part where you want to show the print and create a selection area.

❻マスクをかけるレイヤーをアクティブにします。
6. Make the layer to which you want to add a mask active.

❼「ベクトルマスクを追加」ボタンをクリックします。
7. Click the Add Mask button.

※メニューバー「レイヤー→レイヤーマスク→選択範囲外をマスク」を選ぶ方法もあります。ただし「背景レイヤー」にはマスクをかけることができません。
Alternatively you can choose Layer > Add Layer Mask > Reveal Selection, but you cannot mask the background in this way.

❶「開く」
Open

❷「移動ツール」で移動
Move with the Move tool.

❸「不透明度」を下げる
Lower the opacity

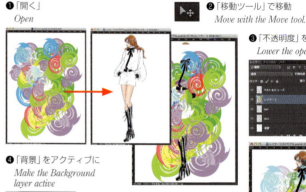

❹「背景」をアクティブに
Make the Background layer active

❺「自動選択ツール」で選択範囲をクリックして選択する
Use the Magic Wand tool to click and make a selection area.

❻マスクをかける「レイヤー」をアクティブに
Make the layer to which you want to add a mask active.

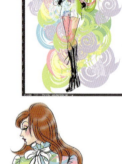

❼「ベクトルマスクを追加」ボタンをクリック
Click the Add Mask button

※マスクされて選択範囲だけが表示される
The mask shows only the selection area.

2) リンクを外す *Unlinking layers*

画像上ではブラウスとショートパンツの形に切り取られたように見えますが、テキスタイルは元の形のまま残っているので、移動させたり変形することができます。
The screen shows a pattern cropped in the shape of the blouse and short pants, but the pattern image remains and keeps the original shape, so it can be still moved and transformed.

❶「リンクアイコン」をクリックして「リンク」を外し、「レイヤーサムネール」をクリックして選択します。
1. Click the Link icon to unlink the layer and the mask, then click the layer thumbnail.

※「リンクアイコン」
Link icon

❶「リンクアイコン」を外して「レイヤーサムネール」を選択
Click the Link icon and select the layer thumbnail.

※「レイヤーサムネール」
Layer thumbnail

■フォトショップで描く

3) 柄位置を自由に移動する　*Changing freely pattern position*

❶不透明度を100%に戻してイメージを確認しながら「移動ツール」でプリントの「レイヤー1」を移動します。
1. Reset the opacity to 100%, then select the Move tool and move the "Layer 1" for the desired position.

上に　*Upward*　　下に　*Downward*　　右に　*Rightward*

❷「レイヤーサムネール」で色を変更、縮小、拡大、変形、描画など自由に変更を加えることができます。
2. On the layer thumbnail, you can freely change the color, scale, transform, draw and so on.

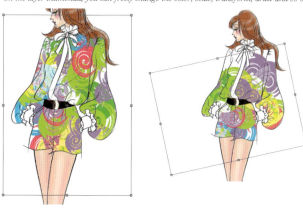

❸「新規レイヤー」を作成しモードを「オーバーレイ」に設定にして、陰影を付けて仕上げます。
3. Create a new layer and set the blending mode to Overlay, then add shades to complete the design.

4) レイヤーマスクの削除と適用　*Deleting and applying a layer mask*

❶「レイヤーマスクサムネール」を「レイヤーを削除」ボタンにドラッグします。「削除」で元の画像に、「適用」でマスク状態で切り抜かれた状態になります。
1. Drag the layer mask thumbnail on the Delete button. Click Delete to restore the original state, or Apply to keep only the masked part.

❶「レイヤーマスクサムネール」をドラッグして「レイヤーを削除」に
Drag the layer mask thumbnail on the Delete

❷「削除」で元画像
Click Delete to restore the original state.

179

■Do Photoshop

「パターンを定義」で連続柄
Masking out Part of an Image with a Layer Mask

1）連続柄の作り方　Creating a repeating pattern

❶メニューバー「ファイル」から「新規」を選択し新規書類を作成します。
1. In the File menu, choose New to create a new document.

　◆書類のサイズ／幅4cm×高さ4cm
　　Document Size/4cm in width and 4cm in height

❷メニューバー「表示→定規」を選択します。
2. In the View menu, choose Rulers.

❸定規の部分にポインタを持っていき、下にドラッグするとガイドラインが表れます。
3. Move the pointer on the ruler and drag inward to display a guide.

❹定規を確認しながら1cmごとにガイドラインを設定します。
4. Set new guidelines at 1cm intervals in accordance with the ruler.

❺ガイドラインに沿って「ブラシツール」で水玉を描きます。
5. Select the Brush tool and create polka dots along the guidelines.

❻「長方形選択ツール」で選択範囲を設定します。
6. Make a selection area with the Rectangular Selection tool.

❼メニューバー「編集→パターンを定義」を選択し新規登録します。
7. In the Edit menu, choose Define pattern to save the selection area.

❽10cm×10cmの新規書類を作成します。
8. Create a new document 10cm width and 10cm height.

❾メニューバー「編集→塗りつぶし」を選択し「カスタムパターン」から新規登録されたパターンを選択します。
9. In the Edit menu, choose Fill and select the newly saved pattern from the Custom Pattern.

　※選択の範囲によってパターンの連続柄が決定されるため、送りに注意して選択します。
　　The selection area determines repeat of the pattern, so make sure of selecting the disired area.

⓫「選択範囲」を中心部からずらして選択すると寸断された部分からの連続柄になります。
11. You can create a pattern with cropped repeat with an off-centered selection area.

❶新規書類を作成
Create a new document.

❷「表示→定規」にチェックを入れると書類の左端と上に目盛が表示
In the View menu, choose Rulers. Rulers appear along the top and left side of the window.

❸目盛部分からドラッグでガイドラインを表示
Drag inward from the ruler to show the guidelines.

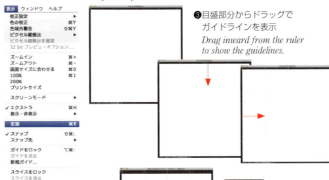

❹目盛を見ながら1cmごとにガイドラインを設定
Set new guidelines at 1cm intervals in accordance with the ruler.

❺ガイドにそってブラシツールで水玉を描く
Create polka dots along the guidelines with the Brush tool.

❻長方形選択ツール
Rectangular Selection tool

❼パターンを定義
Define Pattern

❽新規書類に「パターン」で塗りつぶし
Fill the new document with Pattern.

❾選択範囲を中心部からずらす
An off-centered selection area

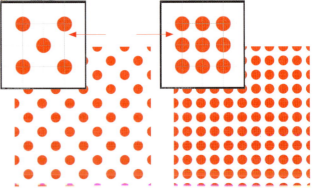

180

2) デザイン画にマッピングする   *Adding the pattern to a clothing image*

❶「ファイル」から「開く」で「パターンを定義モデル1」を開きます。
1. *In the File menu, choose Open to open the "Define Pattern Model 1".*

❷ 新規レイヤーを追加し「長方形選択ツール」で選択範囲を設定します。
2. *Add a new layer and set a selection area with the Rectangular Selection tool.*

❸「編集→塗りつぶし」で新規登録されたパターンで塗りつぶします。
3. *In the Edit menu, choose Fill to fill the selection area with the newly saved pattern.*

❹「背景レイヤー」に戻り「自動選択ツール」で選択範囲をクリックします。
4. *Return to the "Background" and select the clothing area with the Magic Wand tool.*

❺「クイックマスクモード」で選択範囲を確認しながらすべて選択します。
5. *Adjust the selection area using the Quick Mask mode until you see the entire area is exactly selected.*
※細かい部分はブラシで選択します。
   Use a brush to select a small area.

❻ メニューバー「選択範囲」から「選択範囲を反転」を選びます。
6. *In the Selection menu, choose Reverse.*

❼「水玉レイヤー」に戻りキーボードの「delete」キーで削除します。
7. *Return to the polka dot layer and press the Delete key to delete the selection area.*
注) どのレイヤーがアクティブになっているかを確認します。
   Make sure that you are making the correct layer active.

❶ 新規レイヤーに選択範囲を設定して塗りつぶす
   Make a selection area on the new layer and fill it.

❷ 背景レイヤーに戻り「自動選択ツール」で選択部分をクリックする
   Return to the background layer and click the selection area with the Magic Wand tool.

❸ クイックマスクモードで選択範囲を確認する
   Check the selection area with the Quick Mask Mode.

❹ 選択範囲を反転させる
   Reverse the selection area.

選択範囲	フィルター	3D	表
すべてを選択			⌘A
選択を解除			⌘D
再選択			⇧⌘D
選択範囲を反転			⇧⌘I

❺ 反転部分を削除
   Delete the selection area newly made by clicking Reverse.

■ Do Photoshop

「レイヤースタイル」で特殊効果を加える
Masking out Part of an Image with a Layer Mask

「レイヤースタイル」を適用するとワンクリックで、画像にさまざまな特殊効果を加えることができます。また、それらを組み合わせることによって、型押しや織組織のような画像効果も設定することができます。陰影を付けて浮き上がっているように見せる「ドロップシャドウ」や「テクスチャ」など「レイヤースタイル」には10種類のスタイルが用意されています。

You can apply a layer style with a single-click to add multiple special effects on an image. You can also combine several layer styles to create embossing, weaving and other effects on an image. Layer Styles stores 10 styles like Drop Shadow (create three-dimensional effect with shades), Textures and so on.

1）ワンクリックで自在に変更　*Appling easily a change with a single-click*

❶メニューバー「ファイル」から「開く」を選択「レイヤースタイルモデル」を開きます。
1. In the File menu, choose Open?to open the "Layer Style Model".

❷レイヤー「レイヤー1」をアクティブにします。
2. Make the "Layer 1" active.

❸レイヤーパネルの「レイヤースタイルを追加」ボタンをクリックすると、レイヤー効果パネルが表示されます。
3. Click the Add a Layer Style?button in the Layers panel to display the layer effect list.

❹「レイヤースタイル」のダイアログに表示された「グラデーションオーバーレイ」の「グラデーション」をクリックして「グラデーションエディター」を表示します。
4. In the Layer Style dialog box, click the gradient in the Gradient Overlay to open the?Gradient Editor?.

❺「グラデーションエディター」のプリセットでは、選択した時の描画色から背景色で描画されますので、中からイメージのボタンをクリックして決定します。
◆グラデーション名「描画色から背景色へ」
◆グラデーション名「スペクトル」
◆グラデーション名「紫、緑、オレンジ」
◆グラデーション名「イエロー、紫、オレンジ、青」
5. The preset of the Gradient Editor is the foreground and background color, so select the desired gradient.
◆Gradient name: "Foreground to Background"
◆Gradient name: "Spectrum"
◆Gradient name: "Violet, Green, Orange"
◆Gradient name: "Yellow, Violet, Orange, Blue"

❻「レイヤースタイルを追加」すると、レイヤーパネルに効果が表示されます。
6. When you add a layer style, the Layers panel displays the added effect.

※「レイヤー」の右端部分の▲ボタンをクリックすると「効果」の表示部分がレイヤーに格納され再度クリックで表示されます。
You can hide and show the effect list by clicking the triangle at the right side of the layer.

❶「レイヤースタイルモデル」
"Layer Style Model"

❷「レイヤー1」をアクティブに
Make the "Layer 1" active

❸「レイヤー効果を追加」ボタンをクリックすると「レイヤー効果」が表示される
Click the Add a Layer Style button to display layer effects.

❹「グラデーション」をクリック　*Click the "Gradient"*

❺「プリセット」から色を選択
Select a color from the presets.

※▲部分をクリックで表示を格納
Click the triangle to hide the list.

❻レイヤーパネルに「効果」が「目」のアイコンで表示
Click the eye icon to show/hide the effect in the Layers panel.

■フォトショップで描く

2）新規グラデーションを加える *Adding a Set of New Gradients*

❶「プリセット」ではさまざまなグラデーションを置き換えたり加えることができます。
1. You can add multiple gradients or replace already-existing gradients with them in presets.

右上のアイコンをクリックして新規のグラデーションを選択するとダイアログが表示されます。
Click the icon at the top right corner and select a set of new gradients. A dialog box appears.

❷選択したグラデーションを置き換えるか、現在のグラデーションに加えるかを選びます。
2. Add the selected gradients or replace already existing gradients with them.

❸加えられたグラデーションから「スペクトル（標準）」を選択します。
3. Choose the "Normal Spectrum" from the added gradients.

❹任意で作成したグラデーションを新規グラデーションとしてプリセットに加えることができます。
　①分岐点をクリック
　②カラーをクリック
　③新しい色を選択
4. You can add any gradient you create to the presets as a new gradient.
　1) Click the changing point
　2) Click the color
　3) Choose a new color

❺各分岐点のカラーを任意に変更します。
5. You can select any color for each color stop.

❶アイコンをクリックしてダイアログを表示
Click the icon to open a dialog box.

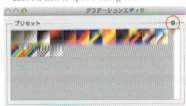

❷「Colorハーモニー1」を加える
Add the "Color Harmony 1"

❸スペクトル標準をクリック
Click the "Normal Spectrum"

①分岐点をクリック
Click the changing point

②カラーをクリック
Click the color

③カラーピッカーで
新しい色を選択
Choose a new color
with the Color
Picker

「新規グラデーション」をクリック
Click New

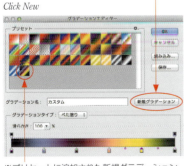

※プリセットに追加された新規グラデーション
Gradient newly added to the presets.

❹「新規グラデーション」をプリセットに追加
Add a new gradient to the preset.

❺各分岐点のカラーを任意に変更
Select any color for each color stop.

※グラデーションを
イメージに合わせて自由に変更
Edit freely the gradient as desired.

183

3) テクスチャを加える *Adding a texture*

❶「レイヤースタイル」の「ベベルとエンボス」にチェックを入れます。
1. Check the Bevel and Emboss box in the Layer Styles dialog box.

❷「テクスチャ」をアクティブにし「パターン」からタイプを選択し、比率と深さを調整します。
2. Check the Texture box and select a pattern, then adjust the scale and depth.

❶▼ボタンをクリック「パターン」を選択
◆ベベルとエンボス／テクスチャ
Click the triangle to select a pattern
◆*Bevel and Emboss/Texture*

❷比率と深さを調節
Adjust the scale and depth

※「ベベルとエンボス」のチェックを外し「パターンオーバーレイ」を適用
Uncheck the Bevel and Emboss box and apply Pattern Overlay

◆サテン
◆パターンオーバーレイ
◆*Satin*
◆*Pattern Overlay*

◆ベベルとエンボス／テクスチャ
◆光彩
◆サテン
◆グラデーションオーバーレイ
（スペクトル）
◆*Bevel and Emboss/Texture*
◆*Glow*
◆*Satin*
◆*Gradient Overlay*
　(Spectrum)

◆ベベルとエンボス／テクスチャ
　（テクスチャの比率を調整）
◆光彩
◆サテン
◆グラデーションオーバーレイ
◆光彩
◆*Bevel and Emboss/Texture*
　(The texture is scaled)
◆*Glow*
◆*Satin*
◆*Gradient Overlay*
◆*Glow*

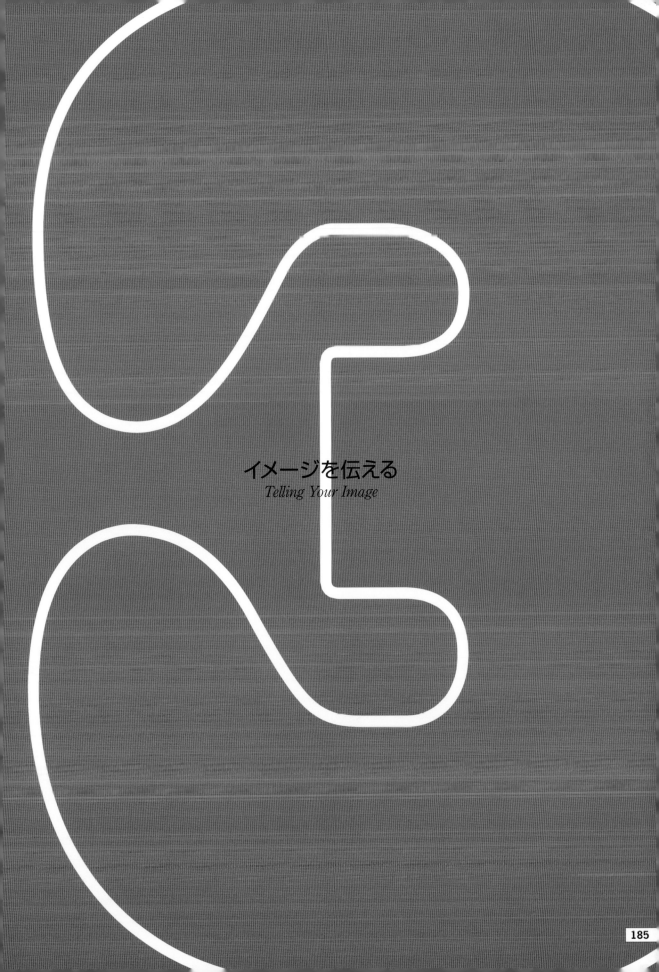

イメージを伝える
Telling Your Image

■ Do Photoshop

「イラストモデル」をレイヤーでカラーバリエーション
Creating Color Variations of a Model Illustration with Layers

1) デザイン画を仕上げる　Completing a design

❶メニューバー「ファイル」から「開く」を選択「企画モデル」を開きます。
1. In the File menu, choose Open to open the "Model Illustration".

❷企画モデルの「レイヤー」を確認します。
2. Check the layers of the model illustration.

❸メニューバー「ファイル」から「開く」を選択「ボーダー」を開きます。
3. In the File menu, choose Open to open the "Horizontal Stripe".

❹「移動ツール」で「ボーダー」をドラッグして企画モデルに移動します。
4. Drag the "Horizontal stripe" with the Move tool and position it on the model.

❺「レイヤー1」のモードを「乗算」にし、メニューバー「編集→変形→自由な形に」を選びます。
5. Set the blending mode of the "Layer 1" to Multiply. In the Edit menu, choose Transform > Free Transform.

❻コントロールポイントをドラッグしてTシャツの形に変形します。
6. Drag control points to transform the stripe along the T-shirt shape.

❼再度「編集→変形→ワープ」を選び、ラインに合わせて立体的に合わせ、オプションバーのOKボタン「○」をクリックして確定します。
7. Open the Edit menu again and choose Transform > Warp. Warp the stripe in perspective along the T-shirt shape and click the circle in the Options bar to complete the transformation.

❽「背景」をアクティブにして「自動選択ツール」を選び、Tシャツの部分でクリックして選択します。
8. Make the "Background" active and choose the Magic Wand tool to click and select the T-shirt part.

❾「レイヤー1」をアクティブにして「選択範囲→選択範囲の反転」を選びます。
9. Make "Layer 1" active and choose Reverse in the Selection menu.

❿キーボードの「delete」を押して選択範囲以外を消去します。
10. Press the Delete key to delete all the part except for the selection area.

⓫再度ボーダーを開き、袖の部分も変形させて仕上げ、レイヤーを「レイヤー1」に統合させ名前を「赤ボーダー」に変更します。
11. Reopen the stripe and transform the sleeve parts to complete the design. Merge the layer into the "Layer 1" and change the layer name to "Red Stripe".

⓬「赤ボーダー」のコピーを作製しメニューバー「イメージ→色調補正→色相彩度」を選択します。
12. Create a copy of the "Red Stripe", then choose Adjustments > Hue/Saturation in the Image menu.

⓭色相のスライダーを動かして色を変更します。
13. Move the hue slider to change the color.

⓮レイヤーのコピーを複製し、色のバリエーションを作製します。
14. Create copies of the layer and make color variations using them.

❶企画モデルを開く
Open the model illustration

❷レイヤーを確認
Check the layers

❸ボーダーを開く
Open the horizontal stripes pattern

❹移動ツールでボーダーをドラッグして企画モデルに移動
Drag and move the stripe on the model illustration with the Move tool

❺編集→変形→自由な形に
In the Edit menu, choose Transform > Free Transform

❻コントロールポイントをドラッグして変形
Drag control points to transform the stripe.

❼ワープで変形「○」で確定
Warp the stripe and finish the transformation by clicking the circle.

❽「背景」をアクティブにし「自動選択ツール」で選択
Make the "Background" active and select the T-shirt part with Magic Wand tool

❾「レイヤー1」をアクティブにし「選択範囲→選択範囲を反転」
Make the "Layer 1" active and choose Reverse in the Selection menu.

❿「delete」で消去　Delete by pressing the Delete key.

⓫袖部分も同様に仕上げ「レイヤー1」に統合
Finish the sleeve parts in the same way and merge them into the "Layer 1".

⓬「レイヤー1」の名前を変更しコピーを作製
Change the name of the "Layer 1" and create a copy of the layer.

⓭色相／彩度／明度のスライダーまたは数値を入力して色を変更
Move the sliders or enter a value in the boxes of hue, saturation and brightness to change the color.

⓮複製コピーを作り色のバリエーションを作成
Create copies and make color variations.

2)「スポイトツール」で同色にする *Selecting the same color with the Eye Dropper tool*

❶「帽子/赤レイヤー」のコピーを作製し「スポイトツール」で「黄ボーダー」の色を吸い取り「描画色」に反映させます。
1. Copy the "Hat/Red" layer, select the Eye Dropper tool and click the yellow of the "Yellow Stripe" to change the foreground color to the yellow.

❷「色相・彩度」ダイヤログボックスの「色彩の統一」にチェックを入れ、「描画色」の色相が反映されます。彩度を100にし明度で調整します。
2. In the Hue/Saturation dialog box, check the Colorize box to display the foreground color hue. Set the saturation value to 100 and adjust the brightness.

❸コピーを複製し、色のバリエーションを作製します。
3. Create copies and make color variations with them.

❹「ヒストリーパネル」の「現在のヒストリー画像から新規ファイルを作製」ボタンをクリックして複製コピーを作製し、画像を統合してバリエーションごとに名前を付けて保存しておくと便利です。
4. It comes very handy to create color variations by clicking Create A New Document From Current State in the History panel to create copies, flatten them and save the new layer created from the flattened copies with a new name.

※元画像はレイヤーを残したまま保存しておきます。
Keep the layers of the original image unflattened.

❶「帽子/赤」のコピーを作製し「帽子/赤」は非表示にしておく
Create a copy of the "Hat/Red" and hide the original "Hat/Red"

とスポイトの先端の色が「描画色」になる
You can select the Eye Dropper tool and click a color to designate a new foreground color

※スポイトで反映された「描画色」
The foreground color selected with the Eye Dropper tool

❷「色彩の統一」にチェックを入れた後、色相と明度を調整
After checking the Colorize box, adjust hue and saturation.

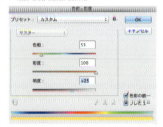

❸複製コピーで他色のバリエーションを作製
Create color variations with the copies.

❹「現在のヒストリー画像から新規ファイルを作製」ボタンをクリックして複製コピーを作り別名で保存
Click Create A New Document From Current State to create copies and save them with a new name.

■ Do Photoshop

「デザイン提案イラスト」作成の手順
Procedure for Creating a Design Proposal Illustration

デザイナーのイメージやデザインのコンセプトを伝えるために、魅力的なマップ作りは欠かせません。マップ作成のポイントは、そのコンセプトに沿った方法を見つけることです。ここでは実際に使用されたプレゼンテーションのための企画マップを作ってみます。一見難しそうですが、今までに使ったことのあるテクニックを効果的に使って仕上げています。

Attractive illustrations are indispensable for designers to present their image or design concept. The point for creating illustrations is to find techniques suited to your concept. In this chapter, we reproduce a design proposal illustration actually created for professional use. It seems difficult, but efficient use of techniques already tried in the previous chapters allows us to complete the illustration.

1) 切り抜きする　*Cropping*

❶ メニューバー「ファイル」から「開く」を選択「提案モデル」を開きます。
1. In the File menu, choose Open to open the "Proposal Model".

❷ レイヤーの表示、非表示でボーダーや帽子の色サスペンダーなどの確認をします。
2. Check the horizontal stripe, hat color, suspender and the others by hiding and showing each layer.

❸「ヒストリーパネル」の「現在のヒストリー画像から新規ファイルを作成」ボタンをクリックして複製コピーを作り、画像を統合します。
3. Click Create A New Document From Current State in the History panel to create a copy and merge the images.

❹「背景」をクリックし、表示されたダイアログボックスでOKして「レイヤー0」にします。
4. Click the "Background" to open a dialog box, then click OK in it to make the background the "Layer 0".

❺「自動選択ツール」で人物以外の背景を選択し「delete」キーで消去します。
5. Select all the part except the person with the Magic Wand tool and delete it with the Delete key.

※マップに使用する画像の1つ1つを用意します。画像解像度が違う時は合わせます。各々別画像にして色を変えたり、切り抜くなどの作業をしておきます。
You should prepare separately all the model images to create the illustration. When the images have different values of resolution, you should set the same value to all of them. These images are used for creating color variations. Cropping and other preparatory operations for these images should be completed before applying them to the illustration.

❶「提案モデルA」
"Proposal Model A"

❷ レイヤーの表示を確認
Check the layers in the Layers panel.

❸ ヒストリーパネルから画像の複製コピーを作成し画像を統合
Create a copy of the image in the History panel and merge the images.

❹ 背景をクリックしてレイヤーに
Click the background to convert it into the "Layer 0".

❺「自動選択ツール」で人物以外の背景を消去して透明セルに
Delete all the areas except for the model using the Magic Wand tool to make them transparent.

※「背景」のままでは透明セルにできないため「レイヤー」に
Convert the background into a normal layer, because you cannot create a transparent area on the background layer.

2) マップを作成する　*Creating a design proposal illustration*

❶メニューバー「ファイル」から「新規」を選択し新規書類を作成します。書類に名前を入力しサイズはA3（420mm×297mm）、解像度は150ppi、カラーモードはRGBカラーに、カンバスカラーは白に設定します。
1. In the File menu, choose New to create a new document. Enter a name for the new file. Set the size to A3 (420 mm by 297 mm), the resolution to 150 ppi, Color Mode to RGB color, and Background Contents to white.

❷「新規レイヤー」を作成します。
2. Create a new layer.

❸「グラデーションツール」を選択し、オプションバーから「カラープリセット」を表示しスペクトルを選択します。
3. Choose the Gradient tool and display the color preset with the Options bar to select the spectrum.

❹開始点から終了点にドラッグして、線形グラデーションで塗りつぶします。
4. Drag from a starting point to an ending point to fill the layer with a linear gradient.

❺レイヤーパネルで「塗り」の数値を下げます。
5. Lower the Fill value in the Layers panel.

※オプションバーにはさまざまな「グラデーションサンプル」があります。いずれも開始点から終了点の位置や長さで距離や角度が変わります。
The Options bar stores multiple gradient samples. Every samples change their length and angle in accordance with the position of the starting point and the ending point and the distance between the two points.

❶新規書類を作成
◆「ファイル名」を記入
◆書類のサイズ／B4（364mm×257mm）
◆解像度／150Pixel/inch
◆カラーモード／RGBカラー
◆カンバスカラー／白

Create a new document
◆*Enter a file name*
◆*Document Size/B4 (364 mm by 257 mm)*
◆*Resolution/150 Pixels/Inch*
◆*Color Mode/RGB color*
◆*Background Contents/White*

❷新規レイヤーを作成
Create a new layer

❸「グラデーションツール」プリセットから「スペクトル」を選択
Select the "Spectrum" in the Gradient tool preset.

❹上から下にドラッグで塗りつぶし
Drag from the top to the bottom to fill the layer.

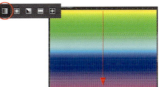

❺レイヤーパネルで「塗り」を下げる
Lower the Fill value in the Layers panel.

※「グラデーション」のオプション　*Gradient options*

円形　　　円錐形　　　反射形　　　菱形
Radial Gradient　*Angular Gradient*　*Reflected Gradient*　*Diamond Gradient*

3) モデルを配置する　*Placing models*

❶「ファイル」から「開く」を選択し「赤ボーダー」を開きます。
1. In the File menu, choose Open to open the "Red Horizontal Stripe".

❷「移動ツール」で「ドラッグ＆ドロップ」し企画マップに移動します。
2. Drag and drop it onto the illustration with the Move tool.

❸メニューバーから「編集→変形→拡大・縮小」で縮小しますが、オプションバーの「縦」「横」の比率を同一にするリンクをクリックして、数値入力で縮小率を入力しておくと便利です。
3. In the Edit menu, choose Transform > Scales to reduce it. It's useful to maintain the aspect ratio by clicking the link icon and before entering a value of scale ratio.

❹他のモデルも同じように開き移動した後、最初の数値入力と同率で縮小させます。
4. Open and move the models in the same way, then enter the same value for their scale ratio to reduce their size.

※各色ボーダーのモデルはあらかじめ、一枚のレイヤーにして切り抜きの処理をしてあります。
Each model of the color variations are already flattened and cropped.

❶「赤ボーダー」
"Red Horizontal Stripe"

❷「移動ツール」でドラッグして移動
Drag and move it with the Move tool

❸「拡大縮小」でモデルを縮小
Reduce their size with Scale.

❹他のモデルもすべて移動し縮小
Move all the other models and reduce their size.

4) マップを作成する　*Creating a design proposal illustration*

❶ボーダーモデルのレイヤーをshiftキーを押しながらすべてアクティブにし「新規レイヤーを作成」ボタンにドラッグして複製コピーを作成します。

1. Hold down the shift key and click all the model layers to make them active. Then drag them onto the Create a New Layer button to create their copies.

❷「レイヤーを結合」で複製されたコピーを統合します。統合されたレイヤーは、一番上のレイヤー名で表示されます。

2. Merge the copies by choosing?Merge Visible. The newly created layer inherit the name of the top layer of the copies.

❸統合された「複製のコピー」は元レイヤーの上に作成されるため、ドラッグして「ボーダーモデル」の下に移動させます。

3. The new layer appears above the original layers of the copies, so move the new layer below the stripe models.

❹メニューバー「編集→変形→拡大・縮小」を選択しコントロールポイントをドラッグし、イメージに合わせて自由に拡大します。

4. In the Edit menu, choose Transform > Scales and drag control points to enlarge the layer to desired size.

❺拡大した「複製のコピー」の描画モードを「通常」から「スクリーン」に変更します。

5. Change the blending mode of the resized layer from Normal to Screen.

※「描画モード」とは
複数の「レイヤー」がある場合、上にある「レイヤー」の画像を、その下にある「レイヤー」にどのように合成して表示させるかを指定するのが「描画モード」です。

What is blending mode?
When there are multiple layers, blending mode designates how the top layer is blended and displayed with all the layers below.

※「描画モード」を使ったときの名称
適用するレイヤーの「描画モード」を「合成色」と呼び、そのすぐ下のレイヤーを「基本色」と呼びます。また、合成後の状態を［結果色］と呼びます。

Color names of the blending mode
The blend color means the color applied on the layer, and the base color means the original color of the layer. The result color means the result of the blend.

❶新規レイヤー作成にドラッグ
Drag them onto Create a New Layer.

❷「表示レイヤーを統合」で複製コピーを統合
Merge the copies with Merge Visible.

❸統合された複製コピーをドラッグしてボーダーモデルの下に移動
Drag and move the merged copies below the stripe models.

❹「拡大・縮小」で変形　*Transform it with Scale.*

❺「描画モード」を変更
Change the blending mode.

「乗算」*Multiply*

「ビビッドライト」
Vivid Light

「スクリーン」*Screen*

「差の絶対値」*Difference*

■フォトショップで描く

5）写真をレイヤーマスクでぼかす　Blurring a Picture with a Layer Mask

❶「ファイル」から「開く」で「観覧車」を開きます。
1. In the File menu, choose Open to open the "Ferris Wheel".

❷「移動ツール」で「企画マップ」にドラッグ＆ドロップして
複製コピーした「ボーダーのコピー」の上に持っていきます。
2. Drag and drop the layer onto the illustration with the Move tool and place it on the "Stripe copy".

❸メニューバー「編集→変形→自由な形に」を選択しコントロールポイントをドラッグし、イメージに合わせて自由に拡大します。
3. In the Edit menu, choose Transform > Free Transform and drag control points to enlarge the layer to desired size.

❹「レイヤー」パネルの「レイヤーマスクを追加」ボタンをクリックします。マスク部分を持たない白地のレイヤーマスクが追加されます。
4. Click Add Layer Mask in the Layers panel. A white layer mask is added without areas of mask.

❺「描画色」を初期設定カラーにします。
5. Set the foreground color to the default color.

❻「グラデーションツール」の「線形グラデーション」を選びます。
6. Choose the Linear Gradient from the Gradient tool options bar.

❼左から右に向かってドラッグします。
7. Drag from the left starting point to the right ending point.

※開始点から終了点までの位置や長さ、ドラッグする角度でマスク範囲が変わります。イメージに合うまで繰り返しチャレンジします。
An area of mask is determined by position of the starting point and the ending point, distance between the two points, and drag direction. Try several settings for the desired result.

※レイヤーマスクを消去する場合は、メニューバー「レイヤー→レイヤーマスク・削除」か、レイヤーのサムネールのマスク部分をゴミ箱にドラッグしダイヤログボックスで確定します。
When you want to delete a layer mask, choose Layer Mask > Delete in Layer menu, or drag the thumbnail of the layer mask onto the trash box. A dialog box appears and complete the delete.

❶「観覧車」 "Ferris Wheel"

❷企画マップに移動
Position it on the illustration.

❸コントロールポイントをドラッグして自由な形に変形
Drag control points to transform freely the layer.

❹「レイヤーマスクボタン」をクリック
Click the Add Layer Mask button.

❺「初期設定カラー」ボタンをクリック
Click the Default colors button.

❻「グラデーションツール」から「線形グラデーション」を選択
Choose Linear Gradient from the Gradient tool options bar.

❼開始点から終了点までドラッグ
Drag from the starting point to the ending point of a gradient.

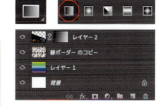

191

「文字ツール」でタイトルを作成する
Creating a Title with the Type Tool

　Photoshopではタイトルの文字を簡単にデザインすることができます。たくさんあるフォントの中からイメージに合わせて選び、サイズ、色、テクスチャーを、少しずつ加工していきます。

You can easily create a title design in Photoshop. You can select various types of font style and change their size, color and texture separately.

1）文字ツールを選ぶ　*Choosing the Type tool*

❶ツールパネルから「文字ツール」を選び、適用したい位置でクリックすると、新規の「テキストレイヤー」が作成されます。
1. Choose the Type tool in the Tools panel and click a point where you want to place letters to create a new text layer.

❷オプションバーの「○」をクリックするか、「テキストレイヤー」をクリックで確定します。
2. Click the circle in the Options bar, or click the text layer in the Layers panel to complete entering the letters.

❸確定後に、オプションバー「テキストサイズ」の▼印をクリックし、文字のサイズを選びます。サイズがない場合は、数値入力で指定します。
3. Click the triangle of the text size box in the Options bar to select the text size. If there is not the desired value, you can enter it in the box.

「フォント」の種類を表示　*Font style*
文字サイズ　*Font size*
文字カラー　*Text color*

❶「テキストレイヤー」
Text layer

❷「○」で確定
「×」で取り消し
Determine with the circle and cancel with the cross.

❸確定後にサイズを選択
After entering the letters, select the size.

■フォトショップで描く

2）フォントの種類を選び効果を加える *Selecting font style and adding effect*

❶オプションバー「フォント」の▼印をクリックしイメージするフォントを選びます。
1. In the Options bar, click the triangle of Font style to select a desired font style.

❷フォントの種類によってサイズは変化しますのでオプションバーの「サイズ」で調節し、「カラー」を選び「OK」ボタンをクリックで確定します。
2. The default font size depends on font style, so adjust the font size in the Options bar. After selecting the color, click OK to finish it.

❸部分的にサイズや色を変更する時は、変更したい文字部分をカーソルでドラッグし、色を選び、同じ操作を行います。
3. With these steps, you can also partially change font color or font size by dragging and selecting the part you want to change.

❹メニューバー「編集→変形→拡大・縮小」でサイズを変更することができます。
4. In the Edit menu, choose Transform > Scales to resize the letters.

❹編集から変形
Transform in the Edit menu.

❺レイヤーパネルの「レイヤースタイルを追加」ボタンをクリックします。
5. Click the "Add a New Layer" button in the Layers panel.

❺レイヤースタイルを追加　*Add a layer style.*

❻「ドロップシャドウ」と「ベベルとエンボス」にチェックを入れ「パターンオーバーレイ」をクリック「パターン」の種類を選択します。
6. Check the Drop Shadow and Bevel and Emboss box and click Pattern Overlay. Select a pattern type in Pattern.

❻「パターンオーバーレイ」でパターンを選択
Select a pattern in Pattern Overlay.
※比率／96・
比率／25
Scale/96, scale/25

※「ドロップシャドウ」の角度や距離、パターンの比率等により効果やサイズが大きく変化します。イメージに合うまで、いろいろな効果を試してみましょう。
The effect and size change greatly in accordance with the angle and distance of Drop Shadow and scale of the pattern. Try different effects for the desired result.

❼「フォント」を変更し、レイヤー効果「境界線」を選択し「サイズ」と「位置」を指定します。
7. Change the Font style and select the Stroke to specify the Size and Position.

❼「境界線」*Stroke*

❽「グラデーションオーバーレイ」をクリックし、グラデーションの種類を選び角度を指定します。
8. Click Gradient Overlay, select a gradient type and determine the angle.

❽「グラデーションオーバーレイ」
Gradient Overlay

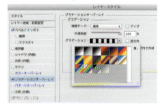

※「カスタムグラデーション」で保存したグラデーションや、「パターンを定義」で保存した写真や絵などは「パターンオーバーレイ」ですべて活用することができます。
You can use all the pictures and paintings saved in Define Pattern and all the gradients saved in Custom Gradient for Pattern Overlay.

※角度／90
Angle/90

※角度／140
Angle/140

193

■ Do Photoshop

「デザイン提案イラスト」を仕上げる
Completing the Illustration

1）バランスを見て完成させる　*Checking the balance to complete the illustration.*

❶全体のバランスや位置を確認しながら「テキストツール」で
タイトル「Amusement park」を打ち込みます。
1. Type the title "Amusement park" with the Type tool and designate the size and position. Make sure of having a balanced title layout.

❷「テキストツール」のオプションバーから「ワープ」を選択し、
ダイアログボックス「スタイル」の中から「円弧」を選びます。
2. In the Options bar of the Text tool, select Warp. Select Arc in the style menu of the dialog box.

❸「円弧」カーブの数値を入力し全体のバランスを見ながら決
定します。
3. Enter a value for Bend. Make sure of having a balanced title layout.

❹メニューバー「レイヤー→レイヤースタイル→レイヤー効果」
または「レイヤー効果を追加」ボタンをクリックし、「レイ
ヤー効果」を加えます。
4. Choose Layer Style > Blending Options in the Layer menu, or click the ?Add a Layer Style button to add layer effects.

❺「ベベルとエンボス」「境界線」「グラデーションオーバーレ
イ」にチェックを入れます。
5. Check the Bevel and Emboss, Stroke and Gradient Overlay box.

❻「グラデーションオーバーレイ→グラデーション」から「プ
リズマ」を選びます。
6. In the Gradient Overlay panel, choose Gradient > Prisma.

❼「境界線」の「サイズ」を調整し「カラー」をクリックして
カラーピッカーで色を選びます。
7. Adjust the size of Stroke and click the Color box to select a color with the Color Picker.

❽レイヤーの右上▼ボタンをクリックし「レイヤーをリンク」
を選び、モデルをリンクさせます。
8. Click the triangle at the right side of the top of the Layers panel. Select Link Layers to link the models.

※「リンク」することでモデルを同時に移動することができ
ます。
Linking allows you to move all the models at once.

❾モデル、背景、タイトルの位置やバランスを見て完成させます。
9. Adjust position and proportions of the models, background and the title to complete the illustration.

❶「テキストツール」でタイトル　*Title typed with the Type tool*

❷オプションで「ワープ」を選択
Select Warp in the Options bar

※カーブ：57%　*Bend: 57%*
※カーブ：26%　*Bend: 26%*

❸「円弧」のカーブ数値入力
Enter a bend value of the Arc.

※全体のバランスを見てカーブを決定
Determine the bend while keeping the balanced layout in the whole image.

❹「レイヤー効果を追加」　*Add a Layer Style.*

❺「レイヤー効果」　*Layer Effects*

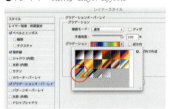

❻グラデーション
オーバーレイ
「プリズマ」
"Prisma" of the Gradient Overlay

❼「境界線」　*Stroke*

❽「レイヤーをリンク」　*Link Layers*

❾全体のバランスを調整　*Adjust general proportions.*

194

■フォトショップで描く

「完成」 Completed illustration

2)「トーンカーブ」で背景のバリエーション　Creating background variations using Curves

● 「トーンカーブ」は画像の明るさやコントラストをカーブの形状で調整
1. Curves allows you to adjust brightness and contrast of an image by changing shape of a curve on a graph.

「イメージ→色調補正→トーンカーブ」
Image > Adjustments > Curves

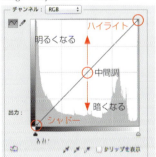

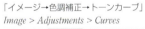

上に
Rise

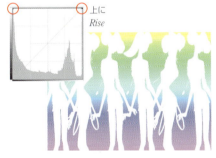

下に
Lower

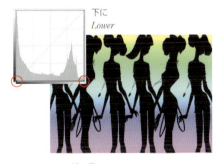

赤に
Reverse

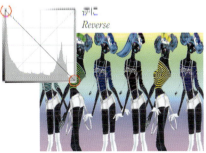

「鉛筆」のアイコンで
カーブを自由に描く
Click the pencil icon to draw a curve freely

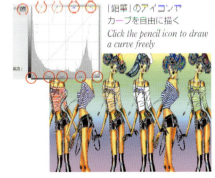

195

■ Do Photoshop

「インビテーション・カード」を作成する
Creating an Invitation Card

※souce: The front cover of "Fashion Message"

スケッチや写真を使ってイメージカードや展示会の案内状も簡単に作成することができます。ここでは墨絵で描いたドローイングを「レイヤーモード」を使ってトレンドカラーに編集しています。

You can also easily create an image card or exhibition invitation card with sketches and pictures. This section describes colorizing an Indian-ink drawing in trend color with the blending mode.

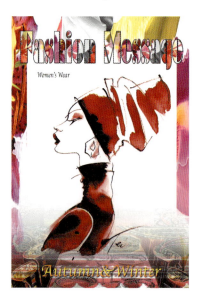

1) インビテーション・カード作成の準備　*Getting ready to create an invitation card*

❶メニューバー「ファイル」から「新規」を開き、プリセットから「ハガキ」を作成します。

1. In the File menu, choose New and designate settings as mentioned at right to create a new document.

❷ファイルから「開く」で「a」を開きカード書類に移動します。

2. In the File menu, choose Open to open the "a" and move it on the created document.

❸メニューバー「編集→自由変形」を選択し画面全体に拡大します。

3. In the Edit menu, choose Free Transform to enlarge the image to fill the screen.

❹メニューバー「イメージ→色調補正→色相・彩度」で色を調整します。

4. In the Image menu, choose Adjustments > Hue/Saturation to adjust the colors.

❺再度「a」を開き「色相・彩度」で色を調整し、全てを選択「編集」から「パターンを定義」で登録しておきます。

5. Reopen the "a" and adjust its colors with Hue/Saturation, then select all the areas and choose Define Pattern in the Edit menu to save it.

❶新規書類を作成
- 「ファイル名」を記入
- 書類のサイズ／ハガキ (100mm×148mm)
- 解像度／300pixel/inch
- カラーモード／RGBカラー
- カンバスカラー／白

❶*Create a new document.*
- *Enter a file name*
- *Document Size/Hagaki (100 mm in width and 148 mm in height)*
- *Resolution/300 pixels per inch*
- *Color Mode/RGB Color*
- *Background Contents/White*

❷「a」を開きドラッグして移動

Open the "a", then drag and move it.

❸「自由変形」で画面一杯に拡大

Enlarge the image to fill the screen with Free Transform.

❹「色調・彩度」で色をイメージ色に調整

Choose Hue/Saturation to adjust the image to the desired color.

※「a」を開く
Open the "a".

※「色調・彩度」で色を調整

Adjust the colors with Hue/Saturation.

❺「編集」から「パターンを定義」で「a」の名前で登録

In the Edit menu, choose Define Pattern to save the image as a pattern named "a".

2) 調整レイヤーで補正　*Adjusting with an adjustment layer*

❶調整レイヤーから「色調補正→レベル補正」を選択します。
1. In the adjustment layer menu, choose Adjustments > Levels.

❷表示された「レベル補正」の操作ウィンドウから「入力レベル」の小さい三角のつまみで画面の明るさを調整しましょう。
2. The Levels panel appears. Adjust the brightness of the image with the small triangle toggle below the Input Levels.

※調整レイヤーは補正効果がレイヤーになっているので、効果の表示・非表示や内容が自由に変更できます。
ただし、下にあるすべてのレイヤーに対して効果が適用されるので、補正をかけたいレイヤーと結合で確定するか、ドラッグで並びを変えて特定のレイヤーに対して補正をかけます。
Adjustment layers contain only an adjustment effect, so it enables you to easily show, hide and edit the effect. However, the adjustment effect is applied to all the layers below the adjustment layer. To apply the adjustment effect to only the layers you want to adjust, you should merge them or change the order of layers.

❸「新規レイヤー」を作成します。
3. Create a new layer.

❹「長方形選択ツール」でイラストモデルを配置するスペースを選択します。
4. Select an area where you want to position the model illustration with the Rectangular Selection tool.

❺「描画色」を初期設定カラーにします。
5. Select the default foreground and background color.

❻「編集」から「塗りつぶし」を選択し、表示されたダイヤログから「背景色」で塗りつぶします。
6. In the Edit menu, choose Fill and select Background Color in the dialog box to fill with it.

※レイヤーに塗りつぶされているためスペースは自由に移動調整できます。
You filled an area of the new layer, so you can freely change its position.

※調整レイヤー
Adjustment layer

❶「レベル補正」を選択
Choose Levels.

❷右の白いつまみを左に移動真ん中のグレーのつまみを右に移動して調整
Move the right white toggle to the left and the middle gray toggle to the right to adjust the brightness.

※レイヤーとして追加された調整レイヤー（レベル補正）
Adjustment layer added as a new layer (named Levels)

❸新規レイヤーを作成
Create a new layer.

❹「長方形選択ツール」でスペースを選択
Select an area with the Rectangular Selection tool.

※初期設定ボタン
Default colors icon

❺描画色と背景色を初期設定
Restore the default foreground and background colors.

❻表示ダイヤログから使用「背景色」を選択し「OK」で塗りつぶす
Select Background Color from the Contents menu in the dialog box and click OK to fill the area.

※塗りつぶされた背景色はレイヤーになっているので位置やサイズを自由に調整
The area filled with the background color is a part of the new layer, so you can freely change its position and size.

■Do Photoshop

3) レイヤーマスクで背景を調整 *Adjusting the background with layer masks*

❶「ファイル」から「埋め込みを配置」で素材「b」を配置し、メニューバー「編集→自由変形」を選択し縮小します。
1. In the File menu, choose Place Embedded to place the image "b", then choose Free Transform in the Edit menu to reduce the image.

❷「レイヤー」パネルの「レイヤーマスクを追加」ボタンをクリックでマスクを追加します。
2. In the Layers panel, click the Add Layer Mask button to add a mask.

❸「描画色」を初期設定カラーにし「グラデーション」ツールの「線形グラデーション」でマスクをかけます。
3. Select the default foreground color and choose Linear Gradient of the Gradient tool to edit the mask.

❹素材「c」も「b」同様に配置し、「自由変形」で縮小、グラデーションでマスクをかけます。
4. Likewise, place the image "c" and "d", resize them with Free Transform and add a mask to them with Linear Gradient.

❶「b」を自由変形で縮小
Reduce the "b" with Free Transform

❷「レイヤーマスク」ボタン
Add Layer Mask button

※マスク部分が黒く表示
A masked area is shown in black.

❸「線形グラデーション」でマスクをかける
Add a mask with Linear Gradient

※マスクのグラデーションで透けて重なったレイヤー
The top layer partially transparent with the gradient mask

❹素材「c」も「b」と同様に縮小しグラデーションでマスクする
Likewise, reduce the "b" and "c" image and apply a gradient mask to them.

4) モノトーンをセピアに調整 *Colorizing a black and white image into sepia-tint*

❶「ファイル」から「埋め込みを配置」で「モデル」を配置します。
1. In the File menu, choose Place Embedded to place the "Model".

❷レイヤーのモードを「乗算」にします。
2. Set the blending mode of the layer to Multiply.

❸メニューバー「イメージ→色相・彩度」のダイアログでセピアの色合いを調整します。
3. In the Image menu, choose Hue/Saturation to colorize the image into sepia-tint in the dialog box.

※モノトーンに色を加えるには先ず「色彩の統一」にチェックを入れます。次に、彩度と明度のスライダーを右に調整し、色相で色味を調整します。
Firstly, you should check the Colorize box to colorize a black and white image. Then, move the saturation and brightness sliders to the right. Finally, adjust the hue to complete the color adjustment.

❹モデルの「レイヤー」を「新規レイヤーボタン」にドラッグして「モデルのコピー」を作成します。
4. Drag the "Model" onto the Create a New Layer button to create a "Model copy".

❶「埋め込みを配置」で「モデル」を配置成
Place the "Model" with Place Embedded.

❷レイヤーのモードを「乗算」に
Set the blending mode of the layer to Mutiply.

❸「色相・彩度」のダイアログを表示し「色彩の統一」にチェックを入れ色相、彩度、明度で調整成
Open the Hue/Saturation dialog box and check the Colorize box. Then adjust the hue, saturation and brightness.

※「色彩の統一」にチェックを入れないと色相は変化しない
When the Colorize box is unchecked, you cannot change the hue.

❹「モデル」をドラッグして「モデルのコピー」を作成
Drag the "Model" to create a "Model copy".

5) タイトルに効果を加える *Adding effect to the title*

❶「文字ツール」でタイトルを打ち込みます。
1. Enter the title with the Type tool.

❷「レイヤースタイルを追加」で「パターンオーバーレイ」を選択し、登録した「a」を選び比率を調整します。次に「ベベルとエンボス」の「境界線」でサイズや境界線の色を設定します。
2. Choose Add a Layer Style to select Pattern Overlay, and select the saved "a" to adjust its scale. Then, check Bevel and Emboss and Stroke to set the stroke size and color.

❸「モデル」のコピーを作成してモードを「乗算」に設定し「モデルのコピー」を、彩度100に調整しています。
3. In this example, a copy of the "Model" is created with Multiply blending mode and 100 saturation, and placed on the original "Model".

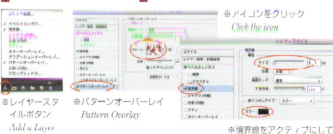

※レイヤースタイルボタン
Add a Layer Style button

※パターンオーバーレイ
Pattern Overlay

❶「文字ツール」でタイトルを打ち込む
Enter the title with the Type tool

※アイコンをクリック
Click the icon

※境界線をアクティブにしてサイズと色を指定
Check the Stroke box and designate its size and color.

❷「レイヤースタイルを追加」でダイアログの「パターンオーバーレイ」でパターンのアイコンから「a」を選択し、「比率」でサイズを決定
Click the Add a Layer Style button to choose Pattern Overlay in the dialog box. Then click the Pattern icon and select the "a" to designate its size with Scale.

※他のレイヤー効果も試してイメージを決定
Try other layer effects for the desired result.

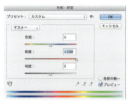

❸乗算にしたコピーの彩度を100にして下にあるモデルと透けて重なる効果を出しています。
Overlapping and transparent effect is created by the copy on the top with the Multiply blending mode and 100 saturation.

※レイヤーの順番
Layer order

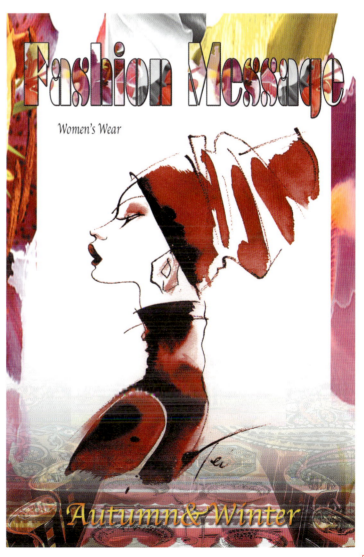

FASHION DRAWING／楽しく描く表現テクニック

2019年9月30日　初版第1刷発行 *(First published September 30, 2019)*

著者⋯⋯⋯⋯⋯⋯⋯⋯鄭　貞子 *Sadako Tei*
(Author)

英訳⋯⋯⋯⋯⋯⋯⋯⋯松本　昴 *Takashi Matsumoto*
(Translated)　　　森田桂泰 *Yoshiyasu Morita*

制作・デザイン⋯⋯⋯佐藤道弘 *Michihiro Sato*
(Production and design)　土屋清了 *Kiyoko Tsuchiya*

発行者⋯⋯⋯⋯⋯⋯⋯佐々木幸二 *Koji Sasaki*
(Publisher)

発行所⋯⋯⋯⋯⋯⋯⋯繊研新聞社 *Senken Shimbun Co., Ltd*
(Publishing office)　〒103-0015 東京都中央区箱崎町31-4
　　　　　　　　　　TEL.03 3661-3681 FAX.03-3666-4236

印刷・製本⋯⋯⋯⋯⋯株式会社シナノパブリッシングプレス
(Printing and binding)　*Shinano Publishing Press Co., Ltd*

無断転載の禁止　本書籍を無断で複写することは、著作権法上での例外を除き
　　　　　　　　禁じられています。

万一乱丁、落丁の場合はお取り替えします。
© SADAKO TEI. 2019 Printed in Japan
ISBN978-4-88124-335-0 C3063